MR. HORACE DINSMORE SR.

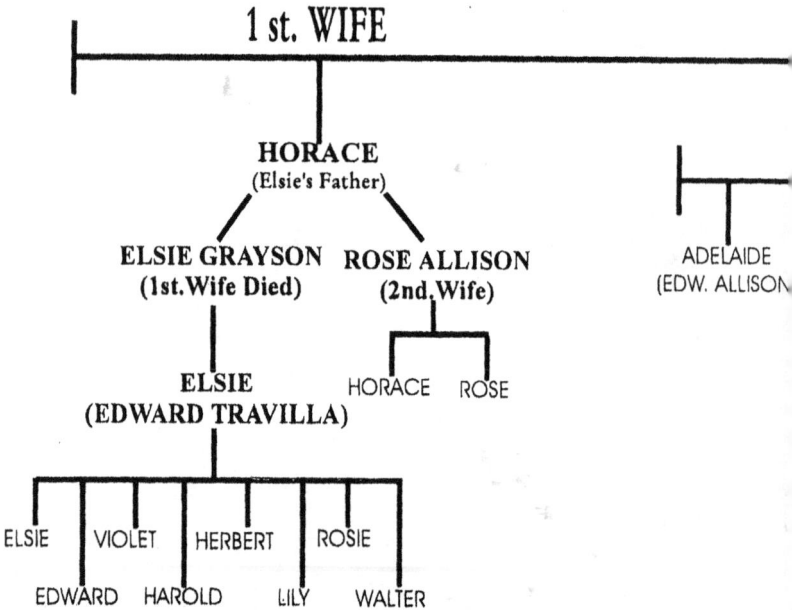

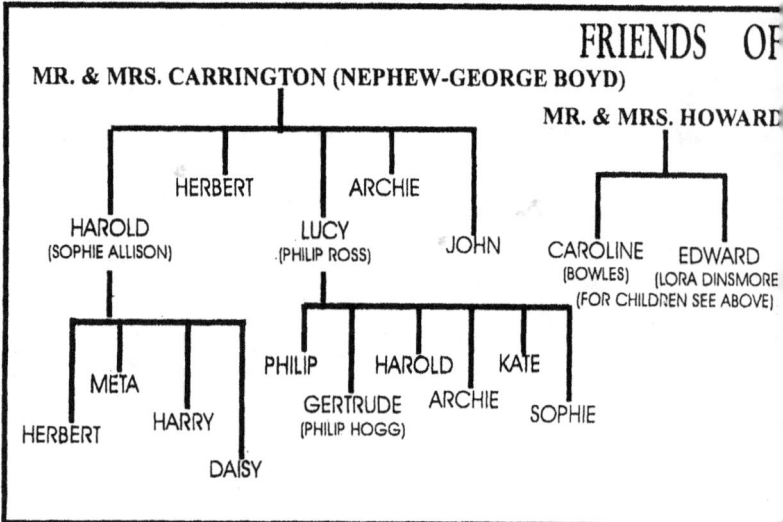

1 st. WIFE

HORACE
(Elsie's Father)

ELSIE GRAYSON
(1st. Wife Died)

ROSE ALLISON
(2nd. Wife)

ADELAIDE
(EDW. ALLISON

ELSIE
(EDWARD TRAVILLA)

HORACE   ROSE

ELSIE   VIOLET   HERBERT   ROSIE

EDWARD   HAROLD   LILY   WALTER

FRIENDS OF

MR. & MRS. CARRINGTON (NEPHEW-GEORGE BOYD)

MR. & MRS. HOWARD

HERBERT   ARCHIE

HAROLD
(SOPHIE ALLISON)

LUCY
(PHILIP ROSS)

JOHN

CAROLINE
(BOWLES)

EDWARD
(LORA DINSMORE)
(FOR CHILDREN SEE ABOVE)

META

PHILIP   HAROLD   KATE

HERBERT   HARRY

GERTRUDE   ARCHIE
(PHILIP HOGG)

SOPHIE

DAISY

MR. HORACE DINSMORE SR.
2 nd. WIFE

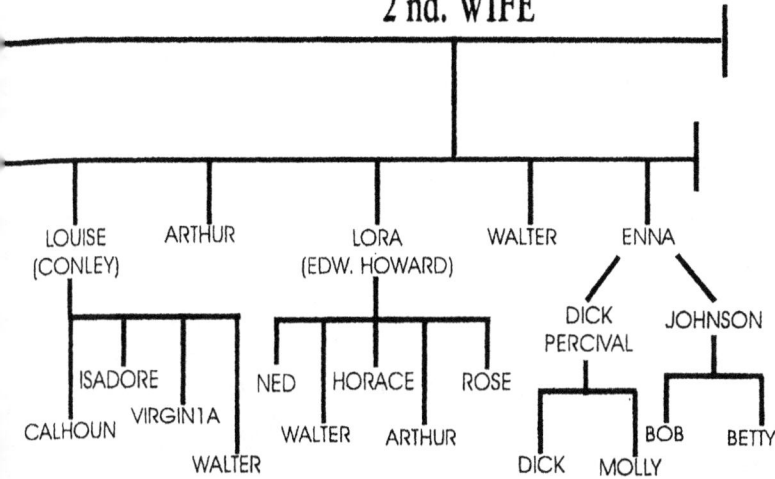

LOUISE (CONLEY) ARTHUR LORA (EDW. HOWARD) WALTER ENNA

DICK PERCIVAL JOHNSON

ISADORE NED HORACE ROSE

CALHOUN VIRGINIA

WALTER ARTHUR

DICK MOLLY BOB BETTY

WALTER

THE FAMILY
MR. & MRS. ALLISON

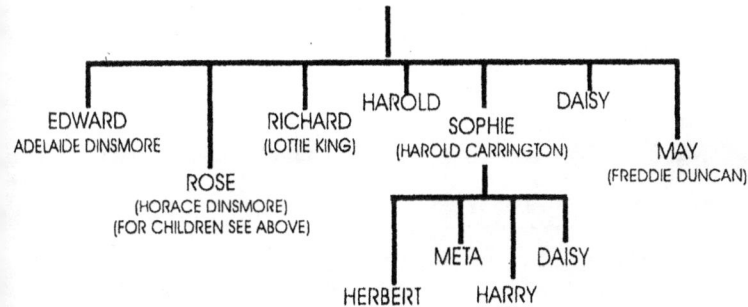

EDWARD
ADELAIDE DINSMORE

RICHARD (LOTTIE KING)

HAROLD

SOPHIE (HAROLD CARRINGTON)

DAISY

MAY (FREDDIE DUNCAN)

ROSE
(HORACE DINSMORE)
(FOR CHILDREN SEE ABOVE)

META DAISY

HERBERT HARRY

Elsie on the Hudson

A SEQUEL TO
Elsie at Home
BOOK 23

BY
Martha Finley

Complete Authorized Edition

ORIGINAL COPYRIGHT 1897, REPUBLISHED 1998
(Protected by Mantle Ministries Press)

Sovereign Grace Publishers, Inc.
P.O. Box 4998
Lafayette, IN 47903
Phone: (765) 429-4122
Fax: (765) 429-4142

A LIST OF THE ELSIE BOOKS AND
OTHER POPULAR BOOKS
BY
MARTHA FINLEY

ELSIE DINSMORE.
ELSIE'S HOLIDAYS AT ROSELANDS.
ELSIE'S GIRLHOOD.
ELSIE'S WOMANHOOD.
ELSIE'S MOTHERHOOD.
ELSIE'S CHILDREN.
ELSIE'S WIDOWHOOD.
GRANDMOTHER ELSIE.
ELSIE'S NEW RELATIONS.
ELSIE AT NANTUCKET.
THE TWO ELSIES.
ELSIE'S KITH AND KIN.
ELSIE'S FRIENDS AT WOODBURN.
CHRISTMAS WITH GRANDMA ELSIE.
ELSIE AND THE RAYMONDS.
ELSIE YACHTING WITH THE RAYMONDS.
ELSIE'S VACATION.
ELSIE AT VIAMEDE.
ELSIE AT ION.
ELSIE AT THE WORLD'S FAIR.
ELSIE'S JOURNEY ON INLAND WATERS.
ELSIE AT HOME.
ELSIE ON THE HUDSON.
ELSIE IN THE SOUTH.
ELSIE'S YOUNG FOLKS.
ELSIE'S WINTER TRIP.
ELSIE AND HER LOVED ONES.

MILDRED KEITH.
MILDRED AT ROSELANDS.
MILDRED'S MARRIED LIFE.
MILDRED AND ELSIE.
MILDRED AT HOME.
MILDRED'S BOYS AND GIRLS.
MILDRED'S NEW DAUGHTER.

CASELLA.
SIGNING THE CONTRACT AND WHAT IT COST
THE TRAGEDY OF WILD RIVER VALLEY.
OUR FRED.
AN OLD-FASHIONED BOY.
WANTED, A PEDIGREE.
THE THORN IN THE NEST.

ELSIE ON THE HUDSON.

CHAPTER I.

CRAG COTTAGE was almost overflowingly full the first night after the arrival of its young mistress and her friends, but with a little contrivance all were comfortably accommodated. Most of them, weary with their journey, slept rather late in the morning, but Captain Raymond and his eldest daughter were as usual out of doors—out in the grounds—early enough to enjoy the beautiful sight of the rising of the sun over the eastern mountains. They met upon the front porch just in time to walk down together to Evelyn's favorite summer house on the edge of the cliff, before the king of day showed his bright face peeping above those eastern heights.

"Oh, what a lovely sight!" exclaimed Lucilla. "I am so glad, papa, that we are out in time to see it."

"Yes," he said, "it is worth the giving up of an extra hour of sleep. Especially as we can take that during the day if we feel the need of it. I would never have you do without needed sleep, daughter. There is nothing gained by it in the end."

"No, papa, but I think I do not need so much as do some others,—Gracie, for instance, —and I do so enjoy these early walks and talks with you—the dearest father that ever any girl had, I am sure," she added, giving him a look of ardent affection.

"Ah, but you must remember there are some fathers you haven't tried," he returned with a slight laugh of amusement, but accompanied by a fond pressure of the pretty white hand she had slipped into his.

"Yet I am just as sure as if I had tried them all, father," she laughed. "There may perhaps be some few nearly as good, but I know they can't be any better. Oh, see! yonder is a yacht coming up the river. I wish it was ours."

"Possibly it may be. Look again," her father said.

" Oh, is it, papa? " she asked eagerly. " Did you order it brought here? "

" I did; and thought it might arrive some time to-day."

" And it is—it is the *Dolphin!* I'm so glad! How nice in you, papa, to have it come to us so soon; for now we can supplement Eva's sleeping accommodations and take delightful little trips up and down the river."

" Yes; that was my idea in having the vessel brought here. There are a number of historical scenes along the Hudson's banks which I have no doubt you and the others would like to visit."

" Oh, yes, indeed, papa! and the very pleasantest way to do it will be in our own yacht— with Captain Raymond to take charge of us and it," she added with a bright smile up into his face. " Oh, the yacht seems to be heading for the little landing down at the foot of the hill! Can't we run down and get aboard of her just to take a peep, here and there, and see that all is right for us to move into the staterooms whenever we will? "

" Yes, come along, daughter. I think we can

go and come back again before the summons to breakfast," he replied, leading the way as he spoke. They reached the landing just as the *Dolphin* had anchored and thrown out a plank to the shore.

"Oh, how bright and fresh she looks!" exclaimed Lulu.

"Yes—outside," laughed her father. "We will go aboard and see whether the same can be said of the inside," he added, leading her carefully onward till they reached the deck.

"Lovely!" she exclaimed as they stepped upon it; "everything is as spick-and-span as possible."

"I am glad indeed that it pleases you, Miss Raymond," said the man in charge, coming hastily forward to greet and welcome them. "I hope you too are satisfied, sir?"

"Perfectly, so far as I have yet examined," returned Captain Raymond in a cheery tone. "You had good weather for your trip up the coast, Mr. Bailey?"

"Yes, sir, yes; indeed, couldn't have asked finer. Hope you all arrived safely and well?"

"Yes, thank you, and I expect to make pretty

constant and good use of the yacht. There could hardly be a better place for it than this river."

"No, sir; I think not."

With Lucilla by his side, the captain went here and there, satisfying himself that everything was in perfect order, exchanging kindly greetings with the sailors, and bestowing words of praise upon their care of the vessel.

"She seems in excellent condition," he said, "and I perceive no dirt or disorder. I should not blush to show her to the highest dignitary in the land."

"I hope not, sir," returned Mr. Bailey with a gratified smile; "and I think if anything were wrong no eyes would detect it sooner than those of her owner."

"Now let us go below, papa," said Lucilla. "I quite want to take a peep into my own cosey stateroom."

"Yes, so you shall," he returned, leading the way.

"Oh!" cried Lulu as they stepped into the saloon; "I see you have been making some changes here, father; and they are all improvements. What lovely carpets and curtains! "

" I am glad you like them," he said with a smile, as she turned toward him with a look of surprise and delight. " The old ones were looking considerably the worse for the wear, and the good parts I knew would be acceptable and useful in another place."

" Oh, yes, I am sure of that," she said in reply, as she hastened to the door of her own little bedroom and threw it open. " Oh, this looks as neat, sweet, and pretty as possible! " she exclaimed joyously. " Can't Gracie and I occupy it to-night, papa? Won't you let us? "

" Probably; if matters are so arranged that your mamma and I, with the younger ones, can be here also. Now," consulting his watch, " we will take a hasty look at the other state-rooms and then hurry back to the cottage on the crag; lest we keep Evelyn's breakfast waiting."

" I am so glad the yacht is here, papa," Lucilla said as they walked up the winding path that led to Crag Cottage. " I felt last night as if it were an imposition for so many of us to crowd into Evelyn's small house—even though we were there by her own invitation; and yet I was afraid she might feel hurt if we should go off very speedily to some house of entertainment."

"Yes," returned her father; "but it will be all right now, I think. If I had known you were so troubled about the matter, I should have told you I was expecting the *Dolphin*."

"But you didn't because you wanted to give me and all the rest a pleasant surprise?" she said questioningly, and with a loving look up into his eyes.

"Yes, that was it. You are as good at guessing as a Yankee."

"But I am a Yankee, am I not?" she laughed.

"Yes; you certainly belong to the universal Yankee nation; as did your ancestors for several generations. Both mine and your mother's were here long before the Revolution."

"A fact which I think is something to rejoice over," she said in joyous tones.

"Therefore something to be thankful for," he said in a tone between assertion and inquiry.

"Oh, yes, sir; yes, indeed! I am very glad

and thankful that you are my father and I am your child."

"And I that you are my own dearly loved daughter," he said in response.

"Ah," as a turn in the walk brought the house into full view, "I see we are no longer the only ones up and about "—for nearly all the guests were now gathered upon the porch or wandering to and fro under the trees or among the flower beds near at hand.

"Oh, yonder come papa and Lu!" shouted Ned at the same moment, starting on a run toward them, quickly followed by his cousins, the Leland boys.

"Good-morning, papa and Lu," "Good-morning, uncle and Lu," cried the three as they drew near, Eric adding: "Have you been down by the river? and is there a walk along down by the water's edge?"

"In some places," his uncle answered, "but you can go down and see for yourselves after breakfast."

"Oh, yes; I presume we can get permission; especially if papa or you will go with us, Uncle Levis."

"It would be still pleasanter to go up and down the river in a boat though," remarked Ned, taking possession of his father's hand as they all moved on toward the house. "Papa, can't you have our yacht brought here for us to go in?"

"I suppose that might be possible," was the smiling rejoinder.

"Oh, that would be splendid, uncle," exclaimed the two Leland boys in a breath.

"Yes," said Ned; "for then we could go every day, and all day, if we wanted to. I mean, if papa and the rest of the grown folks thought best."

But now they had reached the house, and morning greetings were the order of the moment. Everyone was well, in good spirits, and ready to answer with alacrity the summons of the breakfast bell which presently sounded out.

Naturally, their talk turned principally upon the plans for the best manner of spending the next few weeks, in order to gain all possible pleasure and information from their brief sojourn in that part of the country.

"Papa," said Grace, "I should like to see

every place along this river that can boast of
any Revolutionary incident occurring there. I
wish we had our yacht here to travel up and
down in. Won't you please send for it? "

"No, daughter," he said gravely; "I have a
particular reason for not doing so; though I
should like to gratify you."

"Yes, I know you would, father, and so I am
quite satisfied with your decision," she returned
pleasantly, though with a little sigh of regret.

Violet gave her husband a look of surprise,
but made no remark, and the talk went on.

"I think we would all enjoy visiting any and
every place occupied by, or visited by, our Washington," remarked Mrs. Leland.

"Yes," said her husband; "Newburgh, for
one, and it is not so very far away."

"No," said the captain, "that is quite true."

"And there are boats passing up and down
every day, I suppose?" remarked Sydney Dinsmore inquiringly.

"Oh, yes, indeed," said Evelyn; "so we won't
have any difficulty in getting there; though we
can't have the *Dolphin* to go in."

"Papa, why can't we have our yacht come

here so that we can go up and down in it?"
asked Neddie.

"Have I said we couldn't?" was his father's
smiling rejoinder.

"No, sir; at least, I didn't hear you say it—
but she isn't here."

"It is really quite wonderful how much some
little boys know," laughed Lucilla. "However,
I don't believe it would require a great deal of
coaxing to induce papa to send for her."

"But he just refused," said Grace.

"You could telegraph, couldn't you, papa?"
asked Lucilla. "But perhaps the repairs you
said she needed are not finished yet?"

"I think they must be," returned the captain pleasantly. "Perhaps we may get some
news in regard to her to-day."

"And if the repairs are finished, will you
send for her?" asked Violet.

"In case they are, I see no reason why we
should not have the use of her," was the rather
non-committal reply.

CHAPTER II.

A HALF-HOUR later nearly the whole company returned to the front porch as the most attractive spot, since from it was a very fine view of the broad river and its opposite shore.

" Oh," shouted several young voices, " there's our flag! There's Old Glory! "

" And it must be on a boat down close to the landing," added Edward Leland. " May I run down and see, papa? "

" I think you could see quite as well from the summer-house out yonder on the edge of the cliff," replied Mr. Leland, starting for that place himself, followed by most of the others.

" Why it's the *Dolphin*, the *Dolphin!* " exclaimed several voices simultaneously, as they reached the arbor and caught sight of the pretty craft in the river below.

The young people were at once seized with an eager desire to get aboard of her, and, as the captain seemed entirely willing, the parents did not withhold their consent.

"Ah, papa," laughed Grace Raymond, "I understand now why you refused my request to send for our yacht; she was already here, and you wanted to give me a pleasant surprise."

"Yes, daughter, that was just it," he returned; "for I know you like pleasant surprises. And I hope to give you and the rest of our party some pleasant trips up and down the river in her."

"Which I am sure we shall all find extremely enjoyable, captain," remarked Grandma Elsie.

The whole company were wending their way down to the river and the yacht as they talked, and presently they were all on board, viewing and commenting admiringly upon the refurnishing and other improvements.

"Are you all too tired of travel to enjoy a sail—perhaps only a short one—up or down the river?" asked the captain.

"Oh, no—not we, indeed!" was the simultaneous exclamation of many voices, older and younger; and not one was raised against it.

"I see you are all willing," said Captain Raymond, glancing about from one to another of the bright, eager faces. "Suppose I take you to Newburgh, which is not very far away, and let you see the Hasbrouck House, Washington's old headquarters? How many would like that?"

"Oh, all of us! all of us!" cried several voices with enthusiasm.

"Then we will get up steam and go at once," he said. "Will that suit you, my dear?" turning to Violet.

"Perfectly—if we may have a few minutes to go up to the house and make some slight preparation. You see, I have come down without hat or bonnet," she added with merry look and tone.

"Oh, yes, anyone who wishes may do that," he replied pleasantly. "And I must give orders to my cook."

"Oh, no, captain," exclaimed Evelyn, overhearing him; "I have arranged for dinner at the house, and——"

"Then, my dear girl, hurry up and rescind your orders; for we will not be back in season to take that meal here; and the *Dolphin* is well supplied with provisions," was his smiling rejoinder. And with a hasty "Oh, thank you, sir!

You are very, very kind and thoughtful," accompanied by a pleased and grateful look, she hurried away after the others, who were already making rapid progress toward Crag Cottage.

It did not take long to gather up the few articles wanted and return to the yacht, which immediately started for Newburgh.

The weather was all that could be desired—a gentle breeze blowing from the north, and light, fleecy white clouds tempering the heat of the sun.

"How far from New York is Newburgh, papa?" asked Grace.

"Sixty miles," he replied. "It is on the western bank of the river and in the midst of some of the finest scenery in the world, Lossing says, and I entirely agree with him. Are you not of the same opinion, mother?" turning to Grandma Elsie.

"Yes," she said heartily; "and we will have a fine view of it from the piazza of the Hasbrouck House."

"Is that where we are going?" asked Little Elsie.

"Yes; that is the house where Washington

had his headquarters at the close of the Revolution."

"Oh, I'm glad!" exclaimed the little girl.
"I'd like to see every place where Washington
used to be."

"Yes," said her mother; "I think we all
would. But, now, let us not miss the beautiful
scenery we are passing through on our way to
Newburgh."

"Oh, yes, mamma, it is lovely! and I am
proud of it as being part of my country—my
own dear native land."

"As we all are," said Grace. "I think my
native land the best and loveliest the sun shines
upon."

Her father, standing near, smiled his approval of the sentiment, and Grandma Elsie
remarked pleasantly: "That is a good frame of
mind to be in when visiting Revolutionary
scenes."

"This will not be your first visit to Newburgh and the Hasbrouck House, mother?"
said the captain in a tone of inquiry.

"No," she answered, "I was there some years
ago, but am well pleased to repeat my visit."

"When was it that Washington was there?" asked Elsie. "I know that some of the time he was in Massachusetts and at other times in New Jersey and Pennsylvania."

"Yes," said her father, "but he was here on the Hudson, holding his headquarters at Newburgh, at the close of the Revolution. It was in April, 1782, he took possession of his quarters there, and there he continued most of the time until November, 1783, when the Continental Army was disbanded."

"Because the war was over?" asked Eric Leland.

"Yes; and the brave men who had done and suffered so much together had to bid each other farewell, separate, and go to their homes. Of course they were very glad and thankful that liberty was gained and the dreadful struggle over, yet it was sad to part; especially from their beloved chief."

"Wasn't it there, father, that some of them had proposed to make him king?" asked Grace.

"Yes; but he received the proposal with abhorrence. Washington had fought to win freedom for his country, not to win power and glory for himself. He had no hunger for them, but a great love of liberty for his country and himself."

"Do you think he was as great a man as Napoleon, captain?" asked Sydney.

"Greater, much greater! Napoleon undoubtedly had genius, but he was utterly selfish, utterly unscrupulous in the means he took to gain power and satisfy his own ambition—even sacrificing the wife he probably really loved (after his own selfish fashion) in order to get an heir to the throne he had usurped."

"And his fortunes began to wane from the time that he divorced poor Josephine," remarked Mr. Leland.

"Yes; and the son and heir to gain which he had done such wickedness never succeeded to the crown or throne," remarked Grandma Elsie. "'The triumphing of the wicked is short.'"

"I never thought of it before," remarked Sydney; "but isn't it odd that each of those great men married a widow with children, and had none of his own by her?"

"And of our Washington it has been said, 'Providence left him childless that his country

might call him father,' " said Mrs. Leland. " I
have always thought that a very pretty idea."

" A true one too, I do believe," said Evelyn;
" he was so true a patriot—so wise, so unselfish,
so true and good."

" A countryman to be very, very proud of,
and very thankful to God for giving us," said
Grandma Elsie; " especially at that time, when
he was so much needed."

" Are there not a good many places in this
neighborhood where something happened during the Revolution, papa? " asked Grace.

" Yes, a good many. Orange County was
one of the first settled portions of this State,
named in honor of William, Prince of Orange,
afterward King of England. The first settlers
in what is now the town of Newburgh were
Germans. They remained for only a time,
however. They grew dissatisfied, sold out, and
left; some going to Pennsylvania. Their places
were filled by English, Irish, New Englanders,
and a few Huguenots; and a number of settlements were soon planted along the river and in
the rich bottom lands bordering the smaller
streams. Many stirring tales could be told of

their privations, alarms, and sufferings from the attacks of the Indians, both before and during the Revolution."

"Papa," said Little Elsie earnestly, "don't you think we ought to thank our Heavenly Father very often that we didn't live then and here instead of now and where we do?"

"Yes, indeed, daughter," he replied; "we have great reason to thank God for the liberty and security that are ours, and I think we should ever remember with love and gratitude the brave men who fought and bled to secure these liberties for us."

"Indeed we should!" said Mrs. Travilla earnestly. "How it would have cheered and helped them in their toils and privations and struggles if they could have foreseen the great results visible in these days!"

It was not yet noon when they reached Newburgh, pausing in the southern suburbs, where, on a hill overlooking the river, stood a gray old building which the captain pointed out as the Hasbrouck House. They had soon climbed the hill and were standing on the porch, thinking with a thrill of feeling, as they glanced about them and down at the river, that here Washington had stood in days long gone by and gazed upon the same scenes, probably but little changed since then.

Grandma Elsie, the captain, and Mr. Leland had all been there before, and presently pointed out to the others various historic places—Pollopel's Island, Fishkill, New Windsor, Plumb Point, and the Beacon Hills; also, through the gateway in the Highlands formed by Breakneck and Butter hills, glimpse of distant West Point and the mountains that surround it.

Then they went inside the dwelling, passing first into a large square room which they were told was used by Washington as a dining hall and for his public audiences.

"Notice the doors and windows, children," said the captain.

"Windows, papa! why, there is only one!" exclaimed Elsie.

"Ah! and how many doors?" he asked.

"Why, seven!" cried Neddie; "I've counted them."

"Yes, you are right," said his father. "That"—pointing to one on the left— "opens into what was Washington's sitting room; the other, on the same side, into his bedroom."

"There is no plaster on this ceiling," remarked Edward Leland, looking up. "But those great, heavy beams make it look very strong as well as old-fashioned."

"Yes," said Captain Raymond; "they are nine inches wide and fourteen deep. This part of the house is nearly one hundred and fifty years old."

"How much of it, papa?" asked Lucilla.

"This large room and the two bedrooms there on the north side. That part was built in 1750, was it not?" he asked, turning to the woman who had admitted them.

"Yes, sir," she replied. "Some time after the kitchen; that is on the south side. In 1770 they added to the west side. The dates are cut in the stone of the walls."

"What a very big fireplace that is!" remarked Little Elsie—"the largest I ever saw."

"Almost big enough to roast an ox in, I should say," said Edward Leland.

"A small bullock probably," said his father.

" Who owns this house now? " asked the boy, turning to the woman.

" The State of New York," she answered. " It used to belong to the Hasbrouck family, but the State bought it to keep as a relic of the Revolution."

" I am glad they did," said Lucilla. " I think everything that Washington ever used should be kept in memory of him."

" Yes, indeed," assented the woman. Then, leading the way, " And we have a cabinet here of relics of the Revolution which I am sure will interest you."

All were much interested in what she showed them, especially in some muskets, of which she said, " They are some of those bought in France by Lafayette, with his own money, and presented to his own favorite corps of light infantry."

" Oh, that makes them very interesting! " exclaimed Lucilla, her cheeks flushing and her eyes sparkling.

Sydney said inquiringly, " Lady Washington was here with her husband, was she not? "

"Oh, yes," was the reply; "in the summer of 1783; and as she was fond of gardening she had some flower beds out in the grounds."

"That was about at the end of the war," said Sydney.

"Yes," said the captain, "and it was in this old house that Washington wrote his address to the officers of whom we were speaking a while ago, and a circular letter addressed to the Governors of all the States on disbanding the army. They were admirable documents.

"A good many of the troops went home on furlough, and then Washington, having leisure for it, went up the Hudson with Governor Clinton to visit the principal battlefields of the North—Stillwater, Ticonderoga, and Crown Point; also to Fort Schuyler, on the Mohawk.

"He returned here, after an absence of nineteen days, to find a letter from the President of Congress asking him to attend upon that body, then in session at Princeton, N. J. He did so, after waiting a little for the recovery of his wife, who was not well. And while waiting he had, out yonder upon the lawn, an affecting final parting with many of his subalterns and soldiers. That took place upon the day he left to answer the call of Congress."

"Did he return here, captain?" asked Evelyn.

"No; he made his headquarters at West Point for a few days in November, and from there went down to New York City and took possession of it on its evacuation by the British."

Our party passed out upon the porch again, feasted their eyes upon the beauties of the land-scape for a few moments; then, having gener-ously remunerated the woman for her services, returned to the yacht.

Again seated upon the deck, they chatted among themselves, their talk running for the most part upon the scenes through which they were passing and the Revolutionary events connected with them.

The captain pointed out New Windsor, as they passed it, with the remark that it was where Washington established his headquarters on the 23d of June, 1779, and again near the close of 1780, remaining till the summer of 1781.

" Oh, can you point out the house, father? " exclaimed Lucilla.

" No," he replied; " it was a plain Dutch building, long since decayed and demolished."

" Did not Washington go from New Windsor to Peekskill? " asked Grandma Elsie.

" Yes," said the captain. " Oh, yonder is Plum Point also, and of that I have a little story to tell. There, at the foot of that steep bank, there was, in the times we have been talking of, a redoubt with a battery of fourteen guns designed to cover strong *chevaux-de-frise* and other obstructions placed in the river. A little above that battery, and long before it was made, a loghouse used to stand. It belonged to a Scotchman named M'Evers. When thinking of emigrating to America, he asked his servant Mike if he would go with him. Mike, being much attached to him, replied, ' Indeed, gude mon, I'll follow ye to the gates o' hell if ye gang there yersel.' So they came over. The ocean could not be crossed so rapidly in those days as in ours, and their voyage was long and tempestuous. Then the vessel, instead of entering New York Harbor by the Narrows, sailed through Long Island Sound and the East River. At the whirlpool called Hellgate the ship struck upon the Hog's Back with a terrible crash. The frightened passengers—none of them more frightened than Mike—rushed upon the deck. 'What place is it?' he asked. 'Hellgate,' answered a sailor. 'God ha' mercy on me!' groaned Mike; 'I promised my master I'd follow him to the gates o' hell, but I didna say I'd gang through with him.' However, the vessel floated off with the tide, carried its passengers safely into the city, and Mike lived to be a gardener on Plum Point."

"Is that a real, true story, papa?" asked Elsie.

"I think so," he said.

"I suppose," said Grandma Elsie, "some—perhaps all—of you have heard an anecdote in connection with that dining room of the Hasbrouck House—published in the New York *Mirror* for 1834?"

Several voices answered in the negative and urged her to go on and tell it, which she did. "During the Revolution," she said, "a Frenchman named Marbois was secretary of that legation here. Shortly before Lafayette's death he, with the American minister and several of his countrymen, was invited to dine at the house of Marbois. At the supper hour the guests were shown into a room which presented a strange contrast to the elegance of the apartments in which they had spent the evening. There were numerous small doors; one uncurtained small window; a low boarded, painted ceiling with large beams; all together giving it very much the appearance of the kitchen of a Dutch or Belgian farmhouse; and on the table was a repast quite in keeping with the appearance of the room. There was a large dish of meat, uncouth-looking pastry, and wine in bottles and decanters, accompanied by glasses and silver mugs such as seemed but ill-suited to the habits and tastes of modern Paris. 'Do you know where we now are?' the host asked, addressing Lafayette and the other guests. They were too much surprised to answer for a moment. They knew they had somewhere seen something like it before—but where? 'Ah! the seven doors and one window!' Lafayette exclaimed presently; 'and the silver camp-goblets, such as the marshals of France used in my youth. We are at Washington's head-quarters on the Hudson, fifty years ago.' "

"A great deal must have happened in this region during the Revolution," remarked Mrs. Leland. "Haven't you another little story for us, mother?"

"Yes; I was just thinking that the taking of a spy occurred not far from here. At the time that Washington's headquarters were at New-burgh, Generals Greene and Knox had theirs in a house on the New Windsor Road about three miles west from Plum Point; and about a mile farther west was the house of Mrs. Falls. There Governor Clinton had his headquarters. He and his brother were in command of Forts Clinton and Montgomery, among the Hudson Highlands, when the British succeeded in tak-ing them in spite of the desperate defence of the American patriots. It was then General Clin-ton established his headquarters at the house of Mrs. Falls and collected his dispersed troops preparatory to marching to the defence of Kingston. About noon on the 10th of Octo-ber a horseman came riding up into the

camp in great haste. The sentinel challenged
him.

"He replied, 'I am a friend and wish to see
General Clinton.'

"The man was a Tory, bearing a message
from Sir Henry Clinton to Burgoyne, who was
at that time hedged up in Saratoga. This messenger supposed the American forces on the
Hudson to be utterly broken and destroyed;
and, as the British never gave our officers their
titles in speaking of or to them, he thought
General Clinton must belong to the British
Army, so believed himself among his friends.

"He was taken to Clinton's quarters, and
when he was ushered into that officer's presence
he perceived his mistake. 'I am lost!' he exclaimed to himself in a low but audible tone,
and hastily taking something from his pocket,
swallowed it, evidently with some difficulty.
This aroused the suspicions of those about him;
a physician was summoned, and gave the prisoner a powerful dose of tartar emetic."

"Why, grandma, what a foolish fellow he
was to take it!" exclaimed Eric Leland.

"I think it was administered surreptitiously,"

she replied, "in a glass of wine or beer probably, without letting him know their suspicions or intentions. I have been giving you Lossing's version of the affair, but years ago I read another, going rather more into detail. It said the patriots did not let the Tory know their suspicions of him, but, acting as if they thought him all right, invited him to eat with them, and secretly put the tartar emetic in the drink furnished him at the meal; that he grew very sick after drinking it, left the table, and went out of doors. They watched him secretly and saw that after getting rid of what he had eaten he covered it with some chips. When he had gone back to his companions at the table some of them went out, scraped away the chips, and found the silver bullet. Lossing says he (the Tory) succeeded in swallowing it a second time and refused to take another emetic until Governor Clinton threatened to hang him upon a tree and have his stomach searched with a surgeon's knife. At that he yielded, and the bullet presently again appeared.

"It was a curiously wrought, hollow sphere, with a compound screw in the centre; inside of it was a note from Sir Henry Clinton to General Burgoyne, written from Fort Montgomery, telling of their success, and expressing the hope that it might facilitate his (Burgoyne's) operations.

"This made the guilt of the prisoner very clear. He was not allowed to escape, and when, soon afterward, Governor Clinton marched with his troops to the help of the people of Esopus, or Kingston, he took the spy with him; and at Hurley, a few miles from Kingston, they tried, condemned the spy, and hung him on an apple tree near the old church. The British had reached Kingston first, and it was then in flames."

"Oh, what a dreadful thing war is!" sighed Grace. "So many people are killed, and so many others robbed of everything but life."

"It is, indeed, an awful thing," assented Grandma Elsie. "May we of this land never again know anything of its horrors by experience."

CHAPTER III.

THE next day was Sunday. There were several churches within easy walking distance, and Evelyn and her guests all attended the morning services. Toward evening they held a little Bible service of their own on the porch, overlooking the beautiful river. Captain Raymond was, as usual, the leader, being the oldest gentleman and the unanimous choice of those who were to take part.

He selected the third chapter of Proverbs, and had them read it verse about; then made a few remarks.

"'In all thy ways acknowledge him, and he shall direct thy paths.' That is a precious promise," he said; "one to plead and to rest joyfully upon in time of doubt and perplexity such as come to all of us. Thus leaning upon God and his promises, we may be free from care and anxiety; content with our lot in life, because he appoints it. 'Godliness with contentment is great gain.' Lucilla, can you tell us of a Bible saint who had learned this lesson?"

"Yes, sir," she replied, turning over the leaves of her Bible as she spoke. "Here in Phillipians, fourth chapter and eleventh verse, Paul says, 'I have learned in whatsoever state I am therewith to be content.'"

"Yes; and he teaches the same to those he addresses in his other epistles. I see you have a passage ready, mother. Will you please read it to us?"

"Yes," Grandma Elsie said in reply; "here in Hebrews thirteenth chapter and fifth verse, he says, 'Let your conversation be without covetousness; and be content with such things as ye have: for he hath said, I will never leave thee, nor forsake thee.'"

Then Violet read, "'But godliness with contentment is great gain; for we brought nothing into this world, and it is certain we can carry nothing out. And having food and raiment, let us be therewith content.'"

"A Christian may well be content and joyful, even though he have but the bare necessaries of life," remarked Grandma Elsie, "for he may boldly say, 'The Lord is my helper, and I will not fear what man shall do unto me.'"

"No," said Mr. Leland, "those who belong to Jesus need fear nothing; for he will never forsake his own, and he has all power in heaven and in earth."

"How can we know if we belong to him, papa?" asked Eric.

"If we give ourselves to him—truly, honestly, and with purpose of heart to serve him while we have any being—he will accept us for his own; for he says, 'Him that cometh unto me I will in no wise cast out.'"

"'Then will we be Christians and follow Christ—so living, acting, speaking that those who know us will take knowledge of us that we have been with Jesus and learned of him,'" the captain said. "But one who does not walk in the footsteps of Christ—striving to follow his example and do his will—to be like him in temper and spirit, is none of his. But if we have of his spirit, then we become with him sons of God. He is our Brother and God the Father, both his Father and ours. He tells us that he came to save souls. 'For the son of man is come not to destroy men's lives, but to save them.' We must make it our chief business to do his will and win souls for him. That is the commission he gives to each one who professes to love him. He bids them, 'Let your light shine,' 'Go ye into all the world and preach the Gospel to every creature.' 'He that winneth souls is wise,' is another Bible text. Each one of us must feel that this is his or her own work. We are none of us to live for self, but to glorify God and save the souls of our fellow creatures—by bringing them to Christ."

"Yes," said Grandma Elsie, "and we are guilty if we neglect to obey our Father's commands. If we truly love him we will be very earnest and persevering in our efforts to obey. The prophet Daniel tells us, 'They that be wise shall shine as the brightness of the firmament; and they that turn many to righteousness, as the stars for ever and ever.'"

"Grandma," said little Ned Raymond, coming to her side, later in the evening, and looking up at the star-spangled sky, "I'd like to shine

like those beautiful stars for ever and ever. I
wish I knew how to turn many to righteousness. What's the way to do it?"

" To tell them the sweet story of Jesus and
his love," she answered in low, moved tones.
" Tell them how he suffered and died that we
might live. But first you must give your own
self to him."

" I think I have, grandma," he said in low,
earnest tones. " I've tried to do it, asking him
to take me for his very own, and I think he has;
because, you know, he says, ' Him that cometh
unto me I will in no wise cast out.' "

" Yes, dear child, that is his own word
and you need have no fear that he will not
keep it."

" But when and where and how should I tell
about Jesus to others?"

" Ask him to show you when and where—to
teach you what to say and do, and help you
never to be ashamed to own yourself one of his
disciples."

" Like my father," he said. " I am sure he
is never ashamed or afraid to let anybody know
that he loves and serves God. I don't often

hear him tell them, but he acts it out always
and everywhere."

"Yes, I think he does," said Grandma Elsie,
"and it is what we all should do. Remember
Jesus' words, 'Whosoever, therefore, shall be
ashamed of me and of my words, in this adul-
terous and sinful generation, of him also shall
the Son of Man be ashamed, when he cometh
in the glory of the Father with the holy
angels.' "

There was a moment of silence; then Neddie
asked:

"Grandma, do you think it was right for our
soldiers in the Revolution to hang that man for
just having that silver bullet in his pocket?"

"Yes; because success in carrying such mes-
sages from one British officer to another would
probably have cost the lives of very many of
our people, and helped the British to take away
our liberties."

"Oh, yes! So he was as bad as a murderer;
wasn't he?"

"Very much like one, I think. War is a
dreadful, dreadful thing! I hope we may
never have another."

"It's always wicked on one side, but sometimes right on the other; isn't it, grandma?"

"Yes; when life and liberty are in peril it is right to fight for their preservation. Especially when it is not for ourselves only, but for our children and future generations. If our fathers had weakly given up to the tyranny of the British Government, we would not be the free people we are to-day."

"And it was a dreadfully hard fight for them; wasn't it, grandma?" remarked little Elsie, who had drawn near enough to hear the latter part of the conversation.

"It was, indeed; and our poor soldiers went through terrible sufferings, from lack of prompt pay and proper food and clothing, as well as from wounds and exposure to the inclement weather."

"Yes, grandma, I remember it was terribly cold when they crossed the Delaware River and fought the battles of Trenton and Princeton; and, oh, so hot when the Battle of Monmouth was fought!"

"I'm glad our papa and Brother Max didn't have to help fight those battles," said Ned;

"and I hope we'll never have any more wars. Don't you, grandma?"

"I do, indeed, Neddie," grandma answered; "and I hope it may not be long till we come to the time the Bible speaks of where it says, ' And many nations shall come, and say, Come and let us go up to the mountain of the Lord, and to the house of the God of Jacob; and he will teach us of his ways, and we will walk in his paths: for the law shall go forth of Zion, and the word of the Lord from Jerusalem. And he shall judge among many people, and rebuke strong nations afar off; and they shall beat their swords into ploughshares, and their spears into pruning hooks; nation shall not lift up a sword against nation, neither shall they learn war any more. But they shall sit every man under his vine and under his fig tree; and none shall make them afraid for the mouth of the Lord of hosts hath spoken it.' "

"What a good time that will be," said the little girl thoughtfully. "I wish it might come soon. Don't you, grandma?"

"Yes, dear; I do, indeed!" was the sweet-toned reply.

CHAPTER IV.

It was Monday morning, the sun not an hour high, when Captain Raymond, sitting on the *Dolphin's* deck, reading, heard a light footstep approaching, then a sweet-toned voice saying, " Good-morning, my dear father," and, looking up, found Lucilla standing at his knee, her bright eyes gazing lovingly down into his.

" Good-morning, daughter," he returned, taking her hand and drawing her down to a seat by his side, then passing an arm about her waist and giving her the accustomed morning caress. " Did you sleep well? "

" Yes, indeed, papa; from the minute I laid my head upon the pillow till I woke to find it broad daylight."

" I am glad to hear it. It is something that both you and I should be very thankful for."

" And you, papa? did you sleep well? "

" Very; as I hope and believe all on board did. I suppose you left Grace still asleep? "

"Yes, sir; sleeping so sweetly that I took particular pains to move quietly and not wake her."

"That was right," he said. "I want her— my feeble little girl—to take all the sleep she can."

"So do I, father; and I think she has gained a good deal in health and strength since she has had you at home almost all the time to take care of her."

"That's what fathers are for—to take care of the children," he returned with a smile.

"Well, daughter, what would you like to do to-day?"

"Whatever my father bids me," she said with a happy laugh.

"Ah! isn't that a rash choice?" he asked, passing his hand caressingly over her hair and smiling down at her as he spoke.

"No, sir; I think not—considering how wise, kind, and loving my father is."

"What would you think of a trip up to Kingston—to view it as one of the scenes of Revolutionary occurrences?"

"Oh, I should like it very much!" she exclaimed with eager delight. "Do you think of going there to-day, papa?"

"I have been thinking it would answer very well as a sequel to our Saturday's visit to Washington's old quarters at Newburgh. We will make the suggestion at the breakfast table, and see what the rest of our company think of it."

"Oh, I don't believe anyone will think of objecting. I shall be astonished if they do."

"But there are other places some may prefer visiting first, and it will be only polite and kind to let each one express his or her preference."

"And the majority decide, I suppose?"

"That is my idea," he said pleasantly.

"Your ideas are always kind ones, father dear," she responded with a loving look up into his eyes.

"Though occasionally not altogether agreeable to my eldest daughter, eh?" he returned with a smile, and playfully patting the hand which he held.

"Ah, papa, I do not often object by word or look to your decisions nowadays, do I?" she said half-imploringly.

"No, it has been a very rare thing for a very

long while now," he said with a tenderly affectionate look—" so rare that I really believe my
dear eldest daughter has come to have full faith
in her father's wisdom and love for her."

"Indeed, papa, I don't doubt either in the
very least," she exclaimed with an energy that
brought an amused smile to her father's lips and
eyes.

"Good-morning, papa!" cried a sweet child
voice at that moment; "here we come, and
mamma will follow in a very few minutes."
And with that Elsie and Ned came bounding
across the deck to their father's side. He welcomed both with kind greetings and fatherly
caresses.

"Is your sister Grace up yet?" he asked, and
Elsie answered: "Yes, sir; and almost dressed.
She opened her door as I was going by, and
gave me a kiss, and told me to tell papa she
would be ready to go up to breakfast in a very
few minutes!"

"Ah," he said; "I fear she may hurry too
much for her feeble strength. Neddie, boy, go
down to the cabin, knock at your sister's door,
and tell her papa says it is so early yet that she

need not hurry with her dressing. We will wait till she and mamma are quite ready to go up to the house."

"I will, papa," was the ready and cheerful response, as the little fellow turned to obey, but then he paused with the exclamation, "Oh, here they come—both of them!"

The captain rose to exchange morning greetings with his wife and daughter, then all set out for the cottage on the hill.

They found the other guests gathered on the front porch, and when morning salutations had been exchanged they fell into conversation, breakfast being not quite ready. The question was at once proposed how and where they should spend the day, and when the captain told of his plan in regard to that, it was hailed with delight. No one could think of anything better, and it was decided that they would start very shortly after finishing their morning meal.

"Will it be a long voyage, captain?" asked Sydney in a jesting tone.

"Something less than crossing the Atlantic," he returned with becoming gravity.

"It certainly is, captain," Evelyn said with a

smile. Then turning to Sydney, "Kingston is ninety-three miles north of New York."

"Oh, well then, one will not need to burden one's self with much luggage," laughed Sydney.

"So there will be no time consumed in packing trunks," remarked Lucilla.

"I never have any trouble about that. Papa always does it for me," said Grace, giving him a loving look and smile.

"Will we go on shore at Kingston, papa?" asked Elsie.

"Probably," he replied.

"And see the tree the silver bullet man was hung on?" asked Neddie.

"I do not know whether it is still standing or not, my son," replied his father; "and, if so, it probably looks much like other apple trees. "It was not at Kingston he was hanged, however, but at Hurley—a few miles from there."

"Kingston is a very old place, is it not?" asked Violet.

"Yes," said her mother; "it was settled by the Dutch as early as 1663, Lossing tells us, and at first called Wiltwyck—which means wild witch or Indian Witch—on account of the troubles between the settlers and the Indians. A redoubt was built by the Dutch on the bank of the creek near the old landing place, and they called the creek Redoubt Kill, or Creek. Now it is called Rondout—a corruption of Redoubt. Years later, near the close of the century, the population of the town was increased by a valuable addition from Europe—a colony of French Huguenots, who fled from that dreadful persecution begun in 1685 by Louis XIV.'s revocation of the Edict of Nantes."

"What does that mean, grandma?" asked Neddie.

"I will tell you sometime; perhaps while we are going up the river to-day," she answered in kindly tones. "I cannot do it now, for there is the breakfast bell."

They were all seated upon the *Dolphin's* deck very shortly after leaving the table, and in a few moments the yacht was steaming rapidly up the river. Then Neddie, going to his grandmother's side, claimed her promise to explain to him what was meant by an edict—particularly the one of which she had spoken.

"An edict," she said, "is a public decree that

things shall be so and so. The Edict of Nantes
said that the persecution of the Protestants
must stop and they be allowed to worship God
as they deemed right; the revocation of that
edict gave permission to the Romanists to begin
persecution again. Therefore, to save their
lives, the Protestants had to flee to other lands."

"Where did they go, grandma?" asked Eric,
who was listening with as keen an interest as
Neddie himself.

"A great many to England and Germany and
some to this country. It was really a great loss
to France, for they were industrious and skilful artisans—manufacturers of silk, jewelry,
and glass."

"I'm glad some of them did come here," said
Eric. "The massacre of St. Bartholomew was
before that, wasn't it, grandma?"

"Yes; on the 26th of August, 1572; in that
seventy thousand Protestants were butchered
by the Papists in France, by the authority of
the Pope and the king. From that time on,
until 1598, there were terrible persecutions,
stopped in that year by Henry IV.'s issue of the
Edict of Nantes, allowing, as I have told you,

Protestants to worship God according to the dictates of their consciences. That edict remained in force for nearly a century, but was revoked in 1685 by Louis XIV."

"Then the Protestants moved away to escape being killed?" asked Eric.

"Yes," replied Grandma Elsie, "and some of them came up this river and settled on its shores. They found it less hazardous to dwell beside the savage Indians than among the persecuting Papists."

"So they came across the ocean and up this river and settled near Kingston, did they, grandma?" queried Eric.

"They settled in the valley of Ulster and Orange counties," she answered.

"And then they had good times, I hope," said Neddie.

"Not for some time," she answered, "because the Indians were fierce and jealous of the palefaces, as they called the whites. It was not until after the Revolution that they ceased to give trouble to the white settlers, both Huguenots and others. But it was borne with patience and perseverance; and many of their descendants helped in the hard struggle for our independence."

"Fighting the British in the Revolutionary War, do you mean, grandma?" asked Neddie.

"Yes; fighting for freedom. That was the war that made us the great and growing nation that we are to-day. It was a fearful struggle, but God·helped us, and we should never forget to give him thanks for our liberties."

"I hope we won't," said Eric. "Papa says we have more to be thankful for than any other people; and I think so myself."

"As I do," said his grandma; "and my little grandsons are much better off than very many other children, even in this good land."

"Yes, grandma, I know that; papa and mamma often remind me of it; and I do feel thankful for my many blessings; for none of them more than for my dear, sweet grandma," he added with a loving look into her eyes.

"As I do for my dear grandchildren," she returned, giving him a loving smile and softly patting the hand he had laid on her knee.

"Indeed, we all love you dearly, grandma,"

exclaimed Ned. "But, now, please won't you go on and tell us some more? Tell about the Indians, and what they and the white folks did to each other."

"I could not tell all that was done, nor would it be a pleasant story if I could," replied Grandma Elsie. "The Esopus Indians lived on the flats extending northward from the creek for some distance. They did not fancy their white neighbors, and determined to kill them. They fell upon the settlement one day while the able-bodied men were in the field and slew sixty-five persons. The others fled to the redoubt, and the Indians began to build a stockade near it. But a call for help was sent to New York, and the Governor sent troops, who drove the Indians back to the mountains. Not long afterward the Dutch followed the Indians into their fastnesses, destroyed their forts and villages, laid waste their fields, burned their stores of maize, killed many of their warriors, captured eleven of them, and released twenty-two of the Dutch whom they were holding captives. All that led to a truce the next December and a treaty of peace the following May."

"Were the Huguenots there when all that happened, grandma?" asked Eric.

"No; as I have told you, it was the revocation of the Edict of Nantes which drove them from their native land to this foreign shore, and that did not take place until 1685—more than twenty years later."

"Were the Indians all gone from about Kingston by that time, grandma?" asked Eric.

"Oh, no!" she said. "They as well as the Tories gave a great deal of trouble to the Patriots during the Revolutionary War—that hard struggle for freedom. At the time of the Revolution the New York Legislature, then called 'Convention of the Representatives of the State of New York,' migrated from place to place, being compelled to do so by the movements of the enemy, and finally, in February, 1777, took up their quarters in Kingston until May of that year. They were making a Constitution for the State. It proved a very excellent one, and was adopted. And the first session of the legislature of the State was appointed to meet at Kingston in July. So Kingston was the capital of the State when Sir Henry Clinton took the forts in the Hudson Highlands; and because it was the capital he marked it out for special vengeance.

" The British fleet, under Sir James Wallace, came up the river with 3600 men under the command of General Vaughan. The order given them was to scatter desolation in their track; and they obeyed—destroying all vessels on the river and firing from the ships upon the houses of known Patriots. Also small parties landed and desolated whole neighborhoods with fire and sword. They landed near Kingston on the 13th of October in two divisions, each taking a different road to the town, and burning and destroying as they went. They joined upon a gentle eminence and marched into the town,—then but a small village,—began setting the houses on fire, and soon had almost every one laid in ashes."

" Was Kingston only a very little place then, grandma? " asked Eric.

" A town of only three or four thousand inhabitants," she replied. " Some of the people —warned of the approach of the British—had succeeded in hiding their most valuable effects,

but others lost all they had. A large quantity
of provisions and stores was destroyed. After
doing all that mischief, the British—fearing the
American people would gather together and
come upon and punish them for all this wanton
cruelty—hastily retreated."

"Did it do them any good to burn down the
town, grandma?" asked Eric hotly.

"No; there was nothing gained by it."

"And as they burned the town, there are no
Revolutionary houses to be seen there now, I
suppose?"

"A few houses escaped the fire," she said.
"One is the 'Constitution House'—called so
because it was there the Convention met which
framed the Constitution for the government of
the State. I think we will visit it to-day. Perhaps, too, the old graveyard where many of the
Huguenots lie buried. Will we not, captain?"
addressing him as he drew near their little
group, as if interested to learn what was the
topic of her discourse.

"We will visit any spot that you wish
us to, mother," he answered in his pleasant
tones.

"Were you giving the boys a history of Kingston?"

"A slight sketch," she said; "and they want to see the Constitution House; perhaps the old graveyard too."

"Ah! I think we will visit both; certainly, if all our party wish it."

At that, several of the others gathered about them, asking of what places they were speaking; and, on being told, they one and all expressed themselves as desirous to see everything connected with the history of the town to which they were going. So that was what they did on their arrival at Kingston. They remained there for some hours; then returned to their yacht, and greatly enjoyed the trip back to Evelyn's pretty cottage, which they reached in time for tea.

CHAPTER V.

"How many would like to take another trip up or down the river to-morrow?" asked Captain Raymond, as they sat together on the front porch after leaving the tea table.

"Every one of us, I presume, captain," said Grandma Elsie, with a smiling glance from one to another of the eager, interested faces about them.

"Oh, yes; yes, indeed, we would!" exclaimed several voices, Mrs. Leland adding, "We could hardly contrive a more delightful way of spending the time; there are a number of historic spots which would be interesting ones to visit."

"Tarrytown and the other places connected with Arnold's treachery," suggested Violet.

"Fishkill, too, is a historically interesting place," said her mother.

"West Point also," remarked Lucilla. "Papa took Max and me there once, but I should not at all object to going again."

"I think we can visit all the places mentioned within the next few days," said her father; "and we need not decide until tomorrow morning which we will take first."

"In the meantime we may talk the matter over, I suppose, and see what the majority is in favor of?" remarked Lucilla inquiringly.

"I think that would be a good plan," said her father. "Let everyone feel at perfect liberty to give his or her opinion."

"I think we could hardly find a more interesting locality to visit than Fishkill," said Grandma Elsie. "Though perhaps a longer sail may be thought desirable."

"We could supplement it with as long a one as we might find agreeable, by passing on either up or down the river, upon returning from the shore to the yacht," said the captain.

"Why, yes, so we could," said Violet; "and I think it would be very enjoyable."

"Papa, what is there to see at Fishkill? and what happened there in the Revolution?" asked Elsie Raymond.

"Quite a good deal," replied the captain. "Fishkill village lies five miles eastward from

the landing of that name, on a plain near the
foot of the mountains.   Those high mountains
sheltered it from invasion in the time of the
Revolution, and it was chosen as a place of safe
deposit for military stores.   Also for the con-
finement of Tory prisoners and others captured
by strategy or in skirmishes upon the neutral
ground in West Chester.   For a while too a
portion of the Continental Army was encamped
there; also the State Legislature met there at
one time."

"Was the camp in the town, papa?" asked
Grace.

"No; the barracks were about half a mile
south of the village.   The officers had their
quarters at the house of a Mr. Wharton, and the
barracks extended along the road from there to
the foot of the mountains."

"Is not that vicinity the scene of many of
the incidents given in Cooper's 'Spy'?" asked
Mr. Leland.

"Yes," replied the captain.   "Enoch Crosby
was a spy who did good service to his country
in that capacity, and is supposed to have been
the original of Cooper's spy—Harvey Birch.

In the Wharton House, Crosby at one time went through a mock trial by the Committee of Safety, and was then confined in irons in the old Dutch church in the village. It was in the autumn of 1776 he began his career as spy in the service of his country by learning the plans and purposes of the Tories and revealing them to his Whig friends. In that neighborhood, at that time, secret foes were more to be feared than open enemies, but for a long time Crosby mingled with the Tories, learning their plans and purposes, without being suspected by them; they thought him as much an enemy to his and their country as they were themselves. Lossing tells us that while on one of his excursions he asked lodging for the night of a woman who proved to be a Tory; and that from her he learned that a company of Tories was being formed in the neighborhood with the intention of marching to New York and joining the British Army. He seemed delighted with the idea and most anxious to join the company. He gained the confidence of its captain and learned all his plans. It seems that after their talk they retired to bed; but Crosby did not immediately fall asleep. When all had grown quiet, so that there was reason to suppose everyone else was asleep, he rose and stealthily left the house, hastened to White Plains, where lived the Committee of Safety, and told them what he had just learned of the plans of the Tories. He also suggested that they should hold a meeting the following evening and send a band of Whigs to arrest the Tories and himself as though believing him to be one of them. That plan was carried out; they were all made prisoners, taken to Fishkill, and confined in the old stone church. I believe that church is one of the relics of the Revolution which yet remain.

"When the arrested men were taken there the Committee of Safety was already at the Wharton House prepared to try them. They held an examination of the prisoners after which they—Crosby among the rest—were sent back to their prison. Seemingly by accident, he was left alone with the Committee for a few minutes and the plan was concerted by which he might escape.

"At the northwest corner of the church was

a window hidden by a willow. He reached the ground through that, got rid of his loose manacles, sprang out of his concealment, and rushed away past the sentinels with the speed of a deer. The sentinels fired a few shots after him, but missed him in the gloom; and he escaped unhurt to a swamp."

"Oh, that was good!" cried Eric. "Did he have any more such escapes, uncle?"

"Yes; twice after that he was made a prisoner with Tories, but managed to escape each time. At one time Colonel Van Cortlandt was stationed with a detachment of troops on the east side of the Hudson, to watch what was going on upon the Neutral Ground. One day Crosby was with a part of that detachment near Teller's Point and the mouth of the Croton River, when they saw a British sloop of war come sailing up the stream. It cast anchor in the channel opposite. Crosby and six others then went to the Point, where all but one concealed themselves in the bushes, while the other, dressed in infantry uniform, paraded the beach. Of course the officers on the sloop soon saw and determined to capture him. They promptly sent a boat with eleven men to take him. But as the British landed the American ran. They pursued, not thinking of any danger. Then Crosby and his companions began making a noise in the bushes that made it seem as though they were half a regiment; then they rushed out and called on the enemy to surrender—which they did without firing a shot. The next day the stone church at Fishkill held them as prisoners."

"I suppose Crosby was a born American, uncle?" Eric said inquiringly.

"Yes; born in Massachusetts early in January, 1750."

"That would make him twenty-five a few months before the war began. But he did not live in Massachusetts?"

"No; his parents moved to New York while he was still an infant. When he grew up he learned the trade of a shoemaker; but when the war broke out he gave up his trade and shouldered a musket. He was living at Danbury then, and was one of the hundred men who in 1775 marched to Lake Champlain and fought battles in that quarter until Quebec was

stormed. It was after his return from that
expedition that he engaged in the secret
service."

" Being a spy? " queried Neddie.

" Yes; but at length finding that his many
escapes after being taken prisoner by the Whigs
had excited the suspicions of the Tories, he
gave up that work and joined a detachment of
the Continental Army then stationed in the
Highlands."

" I hope he didn't get killed, papa? " said
Little Elsie.

" No; he lived through the war, and for many
years afterward. In 1827 he was in New York
City as witness at a trial in court, and an old
gentleman who knew him introduced him to
the audience as the original of Harvey Birch—
Cooper's spy. That story had been turned into
a play, and was then being performed at one of
the theatres. Notice was given that Crosby had
accepted an invitation to attend the play, and
the house was crowded with an audience who
warmly greeted the old soldier."

" I'm glad they did," said Elsie. " It must
have been pleasant for him, and I'm sure he

deserved it; for he had helped a great deal to get us all free.   Papa, haven't we just the very best country in all the world? "

" So I think," her father answered with a smile; adding, " and that being the case we ought to be the best people in all the world. Don't you think so, daughter? "

" Yes, indeed, papa; and I mean to try."

" Why not go to Fishkill to-morrow? " asked Sydney.

" All in favor of so doing may say aye," said the captain, glancing around upon the small crowd of hearers, big and little.

" Aye! " exclaimed every voice, and that was followed by a ripple of laughter.   As that died down, " We seem to be of one mind," re-marked the captain pleasantly.   " Well, the yacht will be ready to start immediately after breakfast, if the weather is pleasant.   We would hardly wish to go in a storm."

" Oh, no! " exclaimed several voices; " espe-cially as we have plenty of time to wait for a pleasant day."

" Yes," the captain said; " but there is every indication that we will not have to do so—that

to-morrow will prove as fine a day as we could
wish; and I suggest that our young people—and
all older ones who desire plenty of sleep—
should retire pretty soon; for we will need to
rise early if we want abundance of time for our
expedition. The trip on the river will be short,
but we will probably want to spend at least half
the day on shore."

Everyone followed the captain's good advice;
they were all up early next morning and ready
to start on their proposed trip in good season.

The weather proved pleasant, no accident be-
fell any of them, and all enjoyed very thoroughly their visit to Fishkill and its vicinity.
They visited the Verplanck House—interesting
as having been the headquarters of Baron Steuben when the American Army was encamped
near Newburgh, and also as the place where the
celebrated Society of the Cincinnati was organ-
ized in 1783.

"Won't you please tell us something about
Baron Steuben, papa?" asked Elsie Raymond
as they were returning from their visit to the
Verplanck House.

"Yes," replied the captain. "He was a

German soldier, born in Magdeburg, Prussia. His full name was Frederick William Augustus Henry Ferdinand von Steuben. His father was a captain in the army, and he became a soldier when a mere lad. He saw and took part in a great deal of fighting, and in 1762 was made aide to Frederick the Great. He took part in the siege of Schweidnitz, and that closed his military career in his own land. He retired from the army, and was living most comfortably on a salary, while we were struggling for our freedom. In December, 1777, he went to Paris, on his way to visit some English noblemen who were friends of his. In Paris he met the French minister of war, who seems to have been a good friend to America, for, knowing that the great weakness of our army lay in the fact that the men lacked discipline and knew little or nothing of military tactics, he tried to persuade Steuben to come to this country and teach them.

"But very naturally the baron was not willing to sacrifice his income and his honors in order to help a cause that seemed so desperate. Yet at length he yielded to Germain's solicitation

and promises, and decided to come to the help
of the struggling Colonies. He came over on
a French gunboat; having a long stormy passage
of fifty-five days, the vessel taking fire three
times—a very hazardous thing, as there were
1700 pounds of powder on board. Also there
was an attempt to mutiny. However, he finally
arrived safely at Portsmouth, N. H. He had a
warm welcome there, the whole population
going out to receive him."

"And did he go right into our army, papa?"
asked Elsie.

"He wrote at once to Congress offering his
services to the Colonies, saying he had come to
this country because he would serve a nation
engaged in the noble work of defending its
rights and liberties, adding that although he
had given up an honorable title and lucrative
rank, he asked neither riches nor honors. He
called upon Congress, and told them he would
enter the army as a volunteer; if his services
were not satisfactory, or if the Colonies failed
to establish their independence, he was to receive nothing; but if they were successful, and
he remained in the army, he expected to be re-

funded the income he had given up, and remunerated for his services."

"That was a good offer," remarked Eric. "I suppose they accepted it?"

"They did," replied his uncle; "and Steuben went to Valley Forge, where Washington and his army were encamped at that time. When he saw our half-starved, poorly clad soldiers come creeping out of their huts he was astounded, and said 'No European army could be kept together a week in such a state.' But he began his work at once. He did a great work; probably we could never have won our independence without the help he gave us in training our soldiers for the hard struggle necessary to win it. The fine effect of that discipline was seen in the Battle of Monmouth, when Baron Steuben rallied the retreating and disordered troops of Charles Lee like veterans."

"Did he stay in this country till the war was over, papa?" asked Elsie.

"Yes; and as long as he lived. He made New York City his home for several years. I am ashamed to say that Congress refused to fulfil its contract with him to pay him for his services, but he was given grants of land in New Jersey, Pennsylvania, and Virginia. The first he declined to take when he learned that it was the estate of an old Tory who would be left destitute, and in the kindness of his heart he interceded for him. Steuben was very kind-hearted and generous. Lossing gives us some anecdotes illustrative of that. He says that in Newburgh, at the time of the disbanding of the army, Colonel Cochran was standing in the street penniless, when Steuben tried to comfort him by saying that better times would come.

"'For myself,' replied the brave officer, 'I can stand it; but my wife and daughters are in the garret of that wretched tavern; and I have nowhere to carry them, nor even money to remove them.' As Lossing says, 'The baron's generous heart was touched, and, though poor himself, he hastened to the family of Cochran, poured the whole contents of his purse upon the table, and left as suddenly as he had entered.'

"As he was walking toward the wharf a wounded negro soldier came up to him bitterly lamenting that he had no means with which to get to New York. The baron borrowed a dollar, handed it to the negro, hailed a sloop, and put him on board. 'God Almighty bless you, baron!' said the negro as Steuben walked away. Many such stories could be told of the kind-hearted baron."

"What a shame that Congress did not keep the promise it made him when he first came over here!" exclaimed Lucilla.

"Yes; it was a great shame," acknowledged her father; "however, after seven years of delay they allowed him a pension of $2400. Then he retired to his land; he had a whole township near Utica, N. Y. He cleared sixty acres of that, built a loghouse upon it, and made his home there for the rest of his life; though he went to New York every winter. On the 22d of November, 1795, he was making preparation for that yearly visit, when he was stricken with paralysis. Three days afterward he died. In accordance with directions which he had given, he was buried near his house, with his military cloak around him and the star of honor that he always wore on his breast."

"Ah, the dear, good man! I hope he is reaping a great reward in the other world," said Sydney.

"A wish which I think we can all echo from our hearts," responded Grandma Elsie.

CHAPTER VI.

"WE have had a nice day—a very nice one, I think," remarked Elsie Raymond, as they sat on the deck of the *Dolphin* pursuing their homeward way.

"Where are you going to take us to-morrow, papa?"

"That is a question for the majority of the older people to decide," replied the captain, softly stroking her curls—for she was seated upon his knee—and smiling down affectionately into her eyes.

"That means grandma and mamma, and uncle and aunt, I suppose," said the little girl, looking round inquiringly upon them. "Please, dear, good folks, won't you all say what you want?"

"I think we would all be satisfied to go to any one of the many interesting spots on the banks of this beautiful river," replied Grandma Elsie.

"As I do," said Mrs. Leland, "but, since a choice has to be made, I propose that—if no one prefers any other place—we go to West Point to-morrow."

That motion was put to vote, and the decision given in its favor was unanimous.

"Thinking of going there reminds me of Arnold and his treachery," remarked Lucilla. "Can't we go and see the Robinson House, on the other side of the river, papa?"

"I don't know that visitors are admitted to the mansion now, but we can drive past and view the outside and the grounds," replied the captain. "The house is now called Beverly, the dock from which Arnold made his escape Beverly Dock."

"He got into a boat, papa?" asked Neddie.

"Yes; into his barge, which conveyed him to the British ship *Vulture.*"

"Oh, can't you tell us the whole story of it now, papa, and let us go to the place to-morrow?"

"That might be possible," returned the captain, "if no one objects to hearing a rehearsal of the old story."

No one had any objection, and the captain proceeded with the narrative.

" Arnold was a brave, daring, and successful
soldier in the Revolutionary War; one who did
and suffered a great deal to win his country's
freedom, and perhaps if he had been treated
with perfect justice he might never have turned
traitor. He was badly treated by Congress and
by Gates. After that he got into serious trouble
through his own reckless extravagance. He
was deeply in debt and ready to do almost anything for money. He had married into a Tory
family, too, and perhaps they had an influence
in lessening his love for the cause of freedom
and making him willing to betray his country
for the money he coveted—for filthy lucre. He
learned that Sir Henry Clinton so coveted West
Point that almost any sum of money and any
honors would be given the man who should
enable the British to get possession of that post.
He pondered the matter, and resolved to do the
dastardly deed if possible. He had been de-
clining active service on the plea that his
wounds rendered him unfit for riding on horseback. But now his wounds healed rapidly, his
patriotism was freshly aroused, and he was
eager to again serve his bleeding country.

"It was in that way he talked to his friends in Congress,—General Schuyler and others,—men who, he knew, had influence with Washington. He also prevailed upon Robert R. Livingston—a member of Congress—to write to Washington and suggest the giving of the command of West Point to Arnold.

"Then, under the pretence of having private business in Connecticut, he went there, passing through the camp and paying his respects to Washington on the way. But he said nothing about his wish to be appointed to the command at West Point until he again called on his return; then he suggested to Washington that on rejoining the army he would like that post, as suited to his feelings and the state of his health.

"Washington was surprised, but his suspicions were not aroused. So Arnold got command of that post with all its dependencies; that is, including everything from Peekskill to Kings Ferry. His instructions were dated at Peekskill on the 3d of August, 1780. He went at once to the Highlands and established his quarters at Colonel Robinson's house.

"At this time Arnold had been in correspondence with Sir Henry Clinton for eighteen months. Both wrote over fictitious names, and Clinton did not know who his correspondent was; at least, for a great part of the time he was ignorant of his name and character, the letters passing through the hands of Major André. During the previous winter Arnold had had some connection with a British spy—Lieutenant Hele—in Philadelphia, where he had been sent with a pretended flag of truce in a vessel afterward wrecked in the Delaware, when he—Hele—was made prisoner by Congress."

"I think there was something known of Arnold's plot in England at that time; was there not, captain?" asked Mr. Leland.

"Yes," replied Captain Raymond; "and great hopes were built upon it long before it was to take place. Some of the officers who returned to England in 1780 were often heard to declare that it was all over with the rebels; that they were about to receive an irreparable blow the news of which would soon arrive. But they had no more to say on the subject after the account was received of the plot and the discovery of the traitor. To resume: Arnold wrote his letters in a disguised hand and ambiguous style, affixing to them the feigned signature of 'Gustavus.' André signed his 'John Anderson.'"

"He wasn't so bad a man as Arnold, was he, uncle?" asked Eric.

"I think not, by any means," replied Captain Raymond. "He was a fine young man who enjoyed the unbounded confidence of Sir Henry Clinton. He had been an aide-de-camp of the commander-in-chief, and was now adjutant-general of the British Army.

"Before Arnold's trial by a court-martial Clinton had come to the belief that he was his correspondent. That trial made him seem of less value; but when he got command of West Point his traitorous advances to his country's foes assumed increased importance. So their plans were made. Clinton was to send a strong force up the Hudson at the moment when the combined American and French forces should make an expected movement against New York. That last was one of Washington's plans which Arnold had revealed to the British general. It was thought that West Point would be the repository of the ammunition and other stores of the allied armies. It was reported that the French were to land on Long Island, and from there march against New York, while Washington would approach it from the north with the main army of the Americans; and the plan of the enemy was to send up the river at that precise time a flotilla bearing a strong land force. When they reached West Point, Arnold was to surrender to them under pretence of a weak garrison.

"With the view of carrying out that plan, the British troops were so posted that they could be put in motion on very short notice, while vessels, properly manned, were kept in readiness on the Hudson.

"But now Clinton felt it necessary to make certain of the identity of his correspondent; so he proposed a personal conference, and Arnold insisted that Major André should be the one sent. Clinton had already fixed upon André as the most suitable person to whom to intrust that important mission, and so sent him. I do not know that André went unwillingly, but he did not seek the service, though once engaged in it he did his best.

"The love of money seems to have been Arnold's greatest temptation to the treachery of which he was guilty. His first plan was to have the interview with André at his own quarters in the Highlands, André to be represented as a person entirely devoted to the American cause and possessing ample means for gaining intelligence from the enemy. As secret agents were frequently employed to procure intelligence, this was safe ground to go upon. He sent a letter to André telling him of this arrangement, and assuring him that if he could make his way safely to the American outpost above White Plains, he would find no difficulty after that.

"On the east side of the Hudson at that time was a detachment of cavalry under the command of Colonel Sheldon, who had his headquarters, with a part of his detachment, at Salem. Arnold gave him notice that he was expecting a person from New York whom he was to meet at his quarters for the purpose of making important arrangements for obtaining early intelligence from the enemy. Also he asked Sheldon to send him word to the Robinson House when this stranger arrived.

"But the arrangement was distasteful to André, who had no disposition to act as a spy. He therefore wrote a letter to Colonel Sheldon, knowing that it would be put into Arnold's hands. He proposed a meeting with Arnold at Dobbs Ferry, upon the Neutral Ground, on the next Monday, the 11th instant.

"That letter puzzled Colonel Sheldon, because he had never before heard the name of John Anderson, or anything from Arnold about expecting an escort. But he supposed it was from the person expected by the general, therefore enclosed it to him, writing at the same time that he himself was not well enough to go to Dobbs Ferry, and hoped that he would meet Anderson there himself. It was somewhat difficult for Arnold to explain matters to Sheldon so that his suspicions should not be excited, but he seems to have been skilful in deception, and managed to do so. He left his quarters on the 10th, went down the river in his barge to King's Ferry, and passed the night at the house of Joshua Hett Smith, near Haverstraw."

" That Smith was a traitor too, was he not, captain? " asked Evelyn.

" Probably; though there is a difference of opinion on that point; he acted a part in the work of treason, but was perhaps only Arnold's dupe. Early the next morning Arnold proceeded toward Dobbs Ferry, where André and Colonel Robinson were waiting to meet him, but as he drew near he was fired upon and closely pursued by the British gunboats. That, of course, made it necessary to defer the conference.

" Having gone down the river openly, Arnold thought it necessary to make some explanation to Washington, so wrote him a letter in which he mentioned several important matters connected with his command at West Point and incidentally referred to having come down the river to establish signals as near the enemy's lines as possible, that he might receive prompt notice of any fleet or troops coming up the Hudson.

" This letter was dated at Dobbs Ferry, Sep-

tember 11th, and that night he returned to
his quarters at the Robinson House. He desired to have his interview with André as
speedily as possible, because he knew that
Washington was going to Hartford to hold a
conference with the newly arrived French officers, and that the best time to carry out his
plans for betraying his country would be in the
absence of the commander-in-chief. And as
Washington would cross the Hudson at King's
Ferry, it was very necessary that until his departure no movement should be made that
might excite his suspicion.

"Two days after Arnold had returned to his
quarters he wrote again to André telling him
that a person would meet him on the west side
of Dobbs Ferry on Wednesday, the 20th inst.,
and conduct him to a place of safety where the
writer would meet him. 'It will be necessary,'
he added, 'for you to be in disguise. I cannot
be more explicit at present. Meet me if possible. You may rest assured that if there is
no danger in passing your lines, you will be
perfectly safe where I propose a meeting.'

"Arnold also wrote to Major Tallmadge, at

North Castle, instructing him that if a person named John Anderson should arrive at his station, to send him on without delay to headquarters under the escort of two dragoons.

"The house in which Arnold was living at that time had been the property of Colonel Robinson, but was confiscated because he had become a Tory. The two had been corresponding for some time under the pretence that Robinson was trying to recover the property through Arnold. Sir Henry Clinton had sent Robinson up the river on board the *Vulture* with orders to proceed as high as Teller's Point. It is probable that Robinson knew all about Arnold's treasonable plans and purposes. He now wrote a letter to General Putnam asking for an interview with him on the subject of his property, and, pretending that he did not know where Putnam was, he enclosed his letter to him in one addressed to Arnold, requesting him to hand the enclosed to Putnam, or, if that officer had gone away, to return it by the bearer, adding 'In case General Putnam should be absent, I am persuaded, from the humane and generous character you bear, that you will grant me the favor asked.'

" The *Vulture* was then lying six miles below Verplanck's Point, and the letters were sent to the Point under a flag of truce. Arnold went down to that point some hours before Washington was to arrive there on his way to Hartford, and received and read Colonel Robinson's letter. Arnold took Washington and his suite across the river in his barge and accompanied them to Peekskill. He laid Robinson's letter before Washington and asked his advice. Washington replied that the civil authority alone could act in the matter, and he did not approve of a personal interview with Robinson. Arnold's frankness in all this effectually prevented any suspicion of his integrity as commandant of West Point.

" After receiving Washington's opinion in regard to the matter Arnold dared not meet Robinson; but he wrote to him, and in that letter told him that on the night of the 20th he should send a person on board of the *Vulture* who would be furnished with a boat and a flag of truce, and in the postscript he added, ' I expect General Washington to lodge here on Sunday next, and I will lay before him any matter you may wish to communicate.' It was an ingenious and safe way of informing the enemy just when the commander-in-chief would return from Hartford."

"That looked as though he wanted to put Washington in peril," said Lucilla.

"I think it did," said her father. "That letter was sent to Sir Henry Clinton, and the next morning André went to Dobbs Ferry. Clinton had given him positive instructions not to change his dress, not to go into the American lines, not to receive papers, or in any other way act the character of a spy.

"It was expected that Arnold would visit the *Vulture* and there hold his interview with André. But Arnold had arranged a plan which would be safer for himself, though a greater risk for André.

"About two miles below Stony Point lived a man named Joshua Hett Smith, who had been employed by General Robert Howe, when in command of West Point, to procure intelligence from New York. Which—as Howe was a loyal American officer—would seem to be good reason for supposing that Smith was esteemed a patriotic citizen. Lossing tells us that Smith occupied a respectable station in society, and could command more valuable aid in the business in question than any other person. Arnold went to him and told him he wanted his services in bringing within the American lines a person of consequence with valuable intelligence from New York. It would seem that Arnold had resolved not to adventure himself on the British ship, but to have André take the risk of coming on shore that they might hold their contemplated interview. Arnold seems to have expected it to prove a protracted interview, and arranged with Smith to have it take place partly in his house. Therefore Smith took his family to Fishkill to visit friends, and on his return trip stopped at the Robinson house and with Arnold arranged the plan for getting André on shore for the desired interview.

"Arnold gave Smith the usual pass for a flag of truce, and an order on Major Kierse at Stony Point to furnish him with a boat whenever he

should want one, and he directed Smith to go
to the *Vulture* the next night and bring ashore
the person who was expected to be there.

"Smith did not succeed in getting such
assistance as he needed in boatmen, so failed to
visit the *Vulture* at the appointed time. He
sent a messenger to Arnold with a letter telling
of his failure. The messenger rode all night
and reached the Robinson House at dawn.

"Having received the message, Arnold went
down the river to Verplanck's Point and from
there to Smith's.

"At the Point, Colonel Livingston handed
him a letter just received from Captain Sutherland of the *Vulture*. It was a complaint that
some one of the Americans had violated the
rules of war—showing a flag of truce on Teller's
Point, and when in response a boat with another flag was sent off, as soon as it neared the
shore it was fired upon by some armed men who
were concealed in the bushes.

"The letter was signed by Sutherland, but
was in the handwriting of André. Arnold at
once understood that the sight of that handwriting was meant to inform him that André

was on board of the vessel, and, perceiving that, he set to work making arrangements to bring him ashore. He ordered a skiff to be sent to a certain place in Haverstraw Creek, then went to Smith's house. They soon had everything ready except the boatmen to row the skiff. Samuel and Joseph Colquhon were asked to serve, but refused until Arnold threatened them with punishment, when they yielded.

"It was near midnight when at last they pushed off from the shore, and so still that not a leaf stirred in the forests, and there was not a ripple on the water. When they neared the ship they were hailed by the sentinel on its deck. Smith gave some explanation of their errand, and after some rough words was allowed to go on board. He found Captain Sutherland and Beverly Robinson in the cabin. He had a missive for the latter from Arnold, but though addressed to Robinson its contents were evidently meant for André—inviting him to come ashore and assuring him of safety in so doing. Robinson understood it and, I presume, explained it to André. Two passes signed by Arnold, which Smith brought, made still plainer Arnold's wish that André should come ashore. André yielded and went with Smith, who landed him at the foot of a great hill called Long Clove Mountain, about two miles below Haverstraw, on the western side of the river.

" This was the place Arnold had set for the meeting with André, and he was there hidden in the bushes. Smith took André to him, then left them alone together, and for the first time they heard each the other's voice. They were plotting the utter ruin of this land, and the darkness and gloom of the place seemed to suit the nature of the wicked work. They had not finished their conference when Smith returned to give warning that dawn approached and it would be dangerous for them to linger longer. Smith's house was four miles away. Arnold proposed that they should go there to finish their talk, offering André a horse which he called his servant's, though it is altogether probable it had been brought there for this purpose. André reluctantly complied with the request. He did not know that he was within the American lines until he heard the voice of a sentinel near the village of Haverstraw. His uniform was concealed by a long blue surtout, but he knew that he was in real danger because he was within the enemy's lines without a flag or pass. At dawn they reached Smith's house, and at the same moment heard the sound of a cannonade on the river. It was in the direction of the *Vulture*."

" Fired by the Americans, papa, or by the British? " asked Elsie.

" The Americans," replied her father. " It was an attack upon the British ship *Vulture*. Colonel Livingston had heard that she lay so near the shore as to be within cannon shot and had conceived the idea of destroying her, and during the night had sent a party with cannon from Verplanck's Point; and at dawn, from Teller's Point, they opened fire upon the *Vulture;* so severe a one that the vessel's crew raised her anchor and moved down the river.

" Colonel Livingston had asked Arnold for two pieces of heavy cannon for the purpose of destroying the *Vulture*, but on some slight pretence Arnold refused, and Livingston's detachment could bring only one four-pounder to bear upon her.

" Colonel Lamb of West Point furnished the ammunition—but grudgingly, saying that firing at a ship with a four-pounder was, in his opinion, a waste of powder. As Lossing remarks, he little thought what an important bearing that cannonade was to have upon the destinies of America. It drove the *Vulture* from her moorings, and was one of the causes of the fatal detention of André at Smith's house. The *Vulture* was so seriously damaged that had she not got off with the flood tide she would have had to surrender to the Americans. André was anxious and troubled at sight of her retreat, but when the firing ceased his spirits revived. He and Arnold went on arranging their plot, and settled upon the day when it should be consummated.

" André was to go back to New York; the British vessels, carrying troops, were to be ready to come up the river at a moment's notice, and Arnold was to weaken the post at West Point by sending out detachments among the mountain gorges under the pretence of meeting the enemy, as they advanced, at a distance from the works; and that the river might be left free for the passage of the British vessels a link from the great chain at Constitution Island was to be removed. So the enemy could take possession with very little resistance.

"Also Arnold supplied André with papers explaining the military condition of West Point and its dependencies, asking him to place them between his stockings and his feet, and in case of accident to destroy them. He also gave him a pass; then bade him adieu and went up the river in his barge; probably feeling greatly satisfied with the thought that he had at last fully succeeded in carrying out his wicked scheme to betray his country.

"André remained where he was until evening, then asked Smith to take him back to the *Vulture.* Smith refused, saying he was not well—had the ague. Probably, though, it had been caused by the firing upon the *Vulture,* as he was willing to go with André if he would take the land route.

"To that André finally consented, as he had no other means of reaching the vessel. Arnold had persuaded him that in case of taking a land route he would better exchange his military coat for a citizen's dress, and that he did. Both that and the receiving of papers were contrary to the orders of Sir Henry Clinton; but André felt obliged to be governed by the unforeseen circumstances in which he was now placed. He and Smith started on the short journey together, Smith promising to conduct him as far as the lower outposts of the American line.

"A little before sunset, on the evening of September 22d, they crossed King's Ferry, accompanied by a negro servant, and at dusk passed through the works at Verplanck's Point and turned toward White Plains. They had gone as far as Crompond, a little village about eight miles from Verplanck's Point, when they were hailed by a sentinel who belonged to a party under Captain Boyd. That officer asked the travellers many searching questions, and would not be satisfied that all was right until they showed him Arnold's pass. He had a light brought and examined the pass, and, seeing that it was genuine, he gave them permission to go on, after he had apologized for his doubts of them and given them a friendly warning of danger from the Cowboys in the neighborhood.

He advised them on that account to travel no farther till morning; but Smith said their business was urgent and they must make haste to reach White Plains.

"At that the captain went on to speak very strongly of the dangers of the way, till he so aroused the fears of Smith that he was disposed to tarry where they were for the rest of the night. André was not so inclined, and it was some time before Smith could induce him to stay and take lodging in a near-by cottage.

"They occupied the same bed, and Smith afterward told that it was a weary and restless night for André. They left their bed at dawn and again started upon their journey. As they neared Pine's Bridge, Smith assured André that they were beyond patrolling parties, and André at once shook off his depression and talked gaily, discoursing upon arts, literature, poetry, and the common topics of the day. Near Pine's Bridge they separated; Smith went to Fishkill, stopping at the Robinson House on his way to tell Arnold the particulars of his little journey with André and where he had left him.

" Smith and others had advised André not to take the Tarrytown road because of the many Cowboys in that neighborhood, but André, considering them his friends, disregarded the advice, and, in consequence, met his sad fate."

" It was a pity for him, but a good thing for our country," remarked Lucilla.

" Yes," her father said. " On that very morning a little band of seven volunteers went out near Tarrytown to prevent cattle from being driven to New York, and to arrest any suspicious characters who might be travelling that way. A man named John Yerks proposed the expedition the day before, and enlisted several others to take part in the enterprise. They reached Tarrytown early on the day André did. Four of them agreed to watch the road from a hill above, while Paulding, Van Wart, and David Williams were to conceal themselves in the bushes beside the stream and near the post road.

" Eleven days after that, at the trial of Smith, Paulding and Williams told the story of their capture of André. Paulding testified that he, Isaac Van Wart, and David Williams were lying

by the side of the road about half a mile above
Tarrytown and fifteen miles above Kingsbridge,
between nine and ten o'clock on Saturday
morning, the 23d of September. That they
had lain there about an hour and a half, as
nearly as he could recollect, and had seen several persons with whom they were acquainted
and whom they let pass. Presently one of the
young men with him said, 'There comes a gen-
tlemanlike-looking man who appears to be well
dressed and has boots on. You'd better step
out and stop him, if you don't know him.'

"Paulding went on to say that on that he
got up, presented his firelock at the breast of
the traveler, told him to stand, and then asked
him which way he was going. 'Gentlemen,'
said André, 'I hope you belong to our party.'
Paulding asked him what party. He answered,
'The lower party.' Paulding said he did;
then André said, 'I am a British officer, out in
the country on particular business, and I hope
you will not detain me a minute.' Then, to
show that he was a British officer, he drew out
his watch. Upon that Paulding told him to
dismount. 'I must do anything to get along,'

he said, and made a kind of laugh of it, and pulled out General Arnold's pass, which was to John Anderson, to pass all guards to White Plains and below. Upon that he dismounted, and said, 'Gentlemen, you had best let me go, or you will bring yourselves into trouble, for your stopping me will detain the general's business'; and he said he was going to Dobbs Ferry to meet a person there and get intelligence for General Arnold.

" 'Upon that,' continued Paulding, 'I told him I hoped he would not be offended; that we did not mean to take anything from him; and I told him there were many bad people on the road, and I did not know but perhaps he might be one.' Paulding also said that he asked the person his name, and was told that it was John Anderson. He added that if Anderson had not already told that he was a British officer, he would have let him go on seeing Arnold's pass. He also said that he understood the pulling out of the watch to mean to show that he was a British officer; not that he was offering it to his captors.

"Williams too gave his testimony in regard

to the occurrences. 'We took him into the bushes,' he said, 'and ordered him to pull off his clothes, which he did; but on searching him narrowly we could not find any sort of writing. We told him to pull off his boots, which he seemed to be indifferent about; but we got one boot off and searched in it, but could find nothing. But we found that there were some papers in the bottom of his stocking next to his foot; on which we made him pull his stocking off, and found three papers wrapped up. Mr. Paulding looked at the contents, and said that he was a spy. We then made him pull off his other boot, and there we found three more papers at the bottom of his foot, within his stocking. Upon this we made him dress himself, and I asked him what he would give us to let him go. He said he would give us any sum of money. I asked him whether he would give us his horse, saddle, bridle, watch, and one hundred guineas. He said Yes, and told us he would direct them to any place, even if it was that very spot, so that we could get them. I asked him whether he would not give us more. He said he would give us any quantity of dry goods, or any sum of money, and bring it to any place that we might pitch upon, so that we might get it. Mr. Paulding answered, "No; if you would give us ten thousand guineas, you should not stir one step." I then asked the person who had called himself John Anderson if he would not get away if it lay in his power. He answered, "Yes, I would." I told him I did not intend he should. While taking him along we asked him a few questions, and we stopped under a shade. He begged us not to ask him questions, and said that when he came to any commander he would reveal all.

"'He was dressed in a blue overcoat,' Williams went on to say, 'and a tight bodycoat that was a kind of claret color, though a rather deeper red than claret. The buttonholes were laced with gold tinsel, and the buttons drawn over with the same kind of lace. He had on a round hat, and nankeen waistcoat and breeches, with a flannel waistcoat and drawers, boots and thread stockings.'

"North Castle was the nearest military post, and there they took André and delivered both the man and the papers they had found upon him to Lieutenant Colonel Jameson, the officer in command.

" It seems hard to understand how Jameson could be so foolish as to decide as he did, to send the prisoner immediately to Arnold. He knew that some of the papers were in Arnold's undisguised handwriting, and it seems unaccountable that the circumstances under which they had come into his hands should not have opened his eyes to the treachery of that officer. He wrote a letter to Arnold saying that he sent a certain Mr. Anderson forward under the charge of Lieutenant Allen and a guard, Anderson having been taken while on his way to New York; adding, ' He had a passport signed in your name, and a parcel of papers taken from under his stockings which I think of a very dangerous tendency.' He went on to describe the papers and to say that he had sent them to Washington.

" Major Tallmadge, who was next in command to Jameson, was that day on duty farther down the river. When he returned in the evening and heard of the circumstances, he was filled with astonishment at Jameson's folly, and boldly expressed his doubts of Arnold's fidelity. He offered to take upon himself the entire responsibility of acting on the belief of his guilt, if Jameson would consent. But Jameson refused to allow anything that would seem to imply distrust of Arnold.

" Then Tallmadge earnestly begged of him to have the prisoner brought back. Jameson gave an unwilling consent to that, but insisted on forwarding his letter and informing the general why the prisoner was not sent on. That was the letter Arnold received in time to enable him to make his escape to the *Vulture.*

" Jameson at once sent an express after Lieutenant Allen, who had André in charge, directing him to take his prisoner back to headquarters at North Castle.

" When Major Tallmadge saw André, and noticed his manner and gait as he paced the room, he felt convinced that he was a military man and more than ever certain that Arnold was indeed a traitor. He talked the matter over with Jameson and partly convinced him. The result was the removal of André to Colonel

Sheldon's quarters at North Salem, as a more secure place.

"There André wrote a letter to Washington, giving his name and rank and a brief account of the occurrences which had brought him into his present situation. This he handed to Major Tallmadge, who learned with astonishment that his prisoner was the adjutant-general of the British Army.

"The letter was sealed and sent to General Washington, and the prisoner seemed to feel relieved. In obedience to an order from Washington, André was taken to West Point and kept there until the morning of the 28th, when he was conducted to Stony Point and from there, under a strong escort, to Tappan. Major Tallmadge commanded the escort and rode by André's side all the way. He and André were about the same age and held the same rank in their respective armies. They talked on the way as familiarly as possible. André told Tallmadge that he was to have taken part in the attack on West Point if Arnold's plans had succeeded; that he had asked no reward but the military glory to be won by such service to his

king, though he had been promised the rank
and pay of a brigadier-general if he had succeeded. He inquired earnestly of Tallmadge
what would probably be the result of his capture. In reply Tallmadge reminded him of the
fate of the unfortunate Captain Hale.

" 'But you surely do not consider his case
and mine alike?' said André.

" 'Yes, precisely similar, and similar will be
your fate,' replied Tallmadge.

" The prospect of that—the being branded as
a spy—greatly distressed poor André; he
seemed to feel it the very worst part of his sad
fate."

" To be called a spy, papa? " asked Ned.

" Yes; it is an odious name, and in his case
would not have the excuse that it was work
undertaken for the salvation of his country, as
it was in that of Nathan Hale."

" Nathan Hale? Who was he, papa? and
what did he do? "

" I must go on with this story now, and you
shall learn that of Captain Hale at another
time," replied his father.

" Washington now made arrangements for

the security of West Point, then went to the
army at Tappan. There he called together a
board of general officers and directed them to
inquire into the case of André and report to
him, stating in what light they thought the prisoner should be regarded and what his punishment should be. That court was convened at
Tappan on the 29th of September, and Major
André arraigned before it. He made a plain
statement of the facts, acknowledged and con-
firmed the account he had given in his letter
to Washington, confessed that he came ashore
in the night and without a flag, and answered
the question whether he had anything further
to say in regard to the charges against him by
the remark, ' I leave them to operate with the
board, persuaded that you will do me justice.'

" He was sent back to prison while the board
deliberated long and carefully over the question
of his guilt. Their final verdict was that
' Major André, adjutant-general of the British
Army, ought to be considered as a spy from the
enemy, and that agreeably to the law and usage
of nations, it is their opinion that he ought to
suffer death.'

" The next day Washington's approval of the decision was given, accompanied by the order that the execution should take place on the following day at five o'clock P. M."

" What a pity! " exclaimed Grace. " I think I have read that our officers felt sorry for him and would have been glad to spare his life. Was it not so, papa? "

" Yes," the captain said. " There was a general desire on the part of the Americans to save his life, and I think no one desired it more earnestly than Washington, if it could have been done in a manner consistent with his public duty. The only way to accomplish that was by exchanging him for Arnold, and holding the latter responsible for the acts of his victim. A formal proposition of the kind would not answer,—Washington could not make, nor Clinton accept it,—but a plan to attempt such an arrangement was decided upon. A trusty officer of the New Jersey line, Captain Aaron Ogden, was given a packet of papers by Washington containing an official account of André's trial, the decision of the board of inquiry, and André's letter to his general. Ogden was told to choose his escort of men known for their fidelity, then go to Lafayette for further instructions.

"Lafayette was in command of the light infantry and stationed nearest to the British. He instructed Ogden to travel so slowly that he would not reach Paulus Hotel till near night, and he would be invited to stay there till morning. He was then to get into talk with the commandant of the post about this affair of André, and suggest that it would be well to exchange him for Arnold if it could be done.

"It all occurred just as planned: the commandant received Ogden courteously, sent the package across the river, invited him to stay all night, and in the course of conversation André's case was introduced.

"'Is there no way to spare his life?' asked the commandant.

"'If Sir Henry Clinton would give up Arnold, André might be saved,' replied Ogden. 'I have no assurance to that effect from General Washington, but I have reason to know that such an arrangement might be effected.'

"'On hearing that the commandant left the

company immediately, crossed the river, and had an interview with Sir Henry Clinton. It availed nothing, however. Sir Henry at once refused compliance; honor, he said, would not allow the surrender of Arnold—a man who had deserted from the Americans and openly espoused the cause of the king.

"When Ogden mustered his men at dawn the next morning a sergeant was missing. He had deserted to the enemy during the night. There was no time to search for him, and they returned to Tappan without him."

"Did he go over to the British, papa? Oh, what a naughty man!" cried Ned.

"That was what his fellow-soldiers thought," returned the captain with a smile. "But he was really obeying Washington, who wanted him to obtain in that way some very important information. A paper had been intercepted in which was the name of General St. Clair, mentioned in such a way as to excite suspicion that he was connected with Arnold's treason. The sergeant, who was an intelligent man, soon discovered that there was no ground for such suspicion, and that the paper which had excited it was designed by the enemy to fall into Washington's hands and excite jealousy and ill-feeling among the American officers. The papers were traced to a British emissary named Brown.

"Sir Henry Clinton was much distressed on reading Washington's despatch and the letter of André. He summoned a council of officers and it was at once resolved to send a deputation of three persons to the nearest American outpost to open communication with Washington, present proofs of André's innocence, and try to procure his release. General Robertson, Andrew Elliott, and William Smith were the men chosen as the committee, and Beverly Robinson went with them as a witness in the case. Toward noon, on the last of October, they arrived at Dobbs Ferry, in the *Greyhound* schooner, with a flag of truce.

"General Greene had been appointed by Washington to act in his behalf, and was already at the ferry when the *Greyhound* came to anchor. General Robertson opened the conference with great courtesy of manner and flattering words, and was going on to discuss the subject of conference, when General Greene politely interrupted him by saying, 'Let us understand our position. I meet you only as a private gentleman, not as an officer, for the case of an acknowledged spy admits of no discussion.'

"With that understanding the conference was carried on, the British saying what they could in André's favor, but bringing forward nothing that affected the justice of his sentence. Then a letter from Arnold to Washington was produced. It was impudent, malignant, and hypocritical; menaced Washington with dreadful retaliation if André should be executed, prophesying that it would cause torrents of blood to flow, and the guilt of that would be upon Washington. Such a letter could not reasonably be expected to produce any good effect.

"The conference ended at sunset. Robertson expressed his confidence that Greene would be candid in reporting to Washington the substance of what had passed between them, adding that he should remain on board the *Greyhound* all night, and that he hoped that in the morning he might take Major André back with him, or at least hear that his life was safe.

"Robertson was overwhelmed with astonishment and grief when early the next morning he received a note from Greene stating that Washington's opinion and decision were unchanged, and the prisoner would be executed that day.

"Sir Henry Clinton wrote to Washington, offering some important prisoners in exchange; but it was too late.

"André showed no fear of death, but was very solicitous to be shot rather than hanged. He pleaded for that with touching but manly earnestness, importuning Washington in a letter written the day before his death. It was, however, contrary to the customs of war, and Washington, kind-hearted as he was, could not grant his request.

"Major André was executed at Tappan on the 2d of October, 1780, at twelve o'clock. A large detachment of troops was paraded; there was an immense concourse of people present; excepting Washington and his staff, almost all the field officers were there on horseback. There was a strong feeling of pity for the young man, and the whole scene was very affecting. I suppose the general feeling was that he was suffering the punishment that ought, if possible, to have been meted out to Arnold—the traitor."

"I think history says that André went through it all very bravely; does it not, captain?" asked Sydney.

"Yes; there was a smile on his countenance as he walked from the stone-house where he had been confined, to the place of execution, and he bowed politely to several officers whom he knew, they returning it respectfully. He had hoped to be shot rather than hanged, and when he suddenly came in view of the gallows he started backward and made a pause. An officer by his side asked, 'Why this emotion, sir?' André instantly recovered his composure, and answered, 'I am reconciled to my death, but I detest the mode.' Tears came into the eyes of many of the spectators as they saw him take off his hat and stock, and bandage his own eyes. He slipped the noose over his head, and adjusted it to his neck with perfect firmness. He

was then told that he had an opportunity to
speak if he wished to do so. At that he raised
the handkerchief from his eyes, and said, 'I
pray you to bear me witness that I meet my
fate like a brave man.' He had said of the
manner of his death, 'It will be but a momen-
tary pang,' and so it proved, as, on the removal
of the wagon on which he stood, he expired
almost instantly. The body was placed in an
ordinary coffin, and buried at the foot of the
gallows. And the spot was consecrated by the
tears of thousands."

"But it doesn't lie there now?" Sydney said
half in assertion, half inquiringly.

"No; in 1831 it was taken up, carried to
England, and buried near his monument in
Westminster Abbey. But here we are at our
temporary home again, and further talk on
these interesting historical themes must be de-
ferred until our usual gathering together on
the porch for an evening chat," said the captain as the boat rounded to at the wharf below
Evelyn's cottage.

CHAPTER VII.

THE trip on the *Dolphin* had been restful rather than fatiguing, and all were ready when tea was over for further chat upon the interesting historical themes which had engaged their attention through the day.

"Congress rewarded the men who took André prisoner, did it not, papa?" asked Grace.

"Yes; each of them was given a medal and a pension of two hundred dollars a year. Washington wrote of them to Congress in terms of high praise, proposing that they should receive a handsome gratuity for having saved the country from one of the severest strokes that could have been meditated against it. Lossing tells the whole story in his 'Field-Book of the Revolution,' and gives a picture of the medal."

"Oh, that was good!" exclaimed Little Elsie, adding, "Now, papa, I hope you are going to tell us the rest about the traitor Arnold."

"If all wish to hear it," replied her father; and receiving the assurance that such was the case, he proceeded with the story.

"When Arnold left André at Smith's house he went up the river in his barge and directly to the Robinson House; on arriving there spent a little time with his wife and child, then had a talk with his two aides, Majors Varick and Franks, telling them he was expecting important information from New York through a distinguished channel which he had just opened. This was on the 22d; the day fixed upon for the ascent of the river by the British ships was the 24th, and West Point was to be surrendered to them on their arrival there."

"And they listened to it all and never suspected him?" exclaimed Sydney.

"Yes," said the captain; "he told it all as calmly as if there were no guilt on his soul, and so he appeared on the very day that his treason was to be consummated.

"Washington returned from Hartford two days sooner than Arnold had expected. He passed the night at Fishkill, and he and his suite were in the saddle before dawn, as he was anxious to reach Arnold's quarters before breakfast time, and they had eighteen miles to ride. Men were sent ahead with the baggage and a notice of Washington's intention of breakfasting there; but when the general and his party came opposite West Point, he turned his horse down a lane toward the river.

"Lafayette said, 'General, you are going in a wrong direction; you know Mrs. Arnold is waiting breakfast for us; and that road will take us out of the way.'

"Washington answered good-naturedly: 'Ah, I know you young men are all in love with Mrs. Arnold, and wish to get where she is as soon as possible. You may go and take your breakfast with her, and tell her not to wait for me; for I must ride down and examine the redoubts on this side of the river, and will be there in a short time.'

"But the officers did not leave him, except two aides-de-camp who rode on ahead to explain the cause of the delay. Breakfast was waiting when they arrived, and they all sat down to their meal.

"Arnold seemed moody. Washington had

come back too soon to suit his plans, and the
British had not come up the river at the appointed time. He did not understand it, for
he had not yet heard that André was a prisoner. But before the meal was over Lieutenant Allen came with a letter for him. Arnold
broke the seal hastily, for he recognized Colonel Jameson's handwriting in the address.
Doubtless Arnold expected it would inform him
that the enemy was moving up the river; but instead it told that Major André of the British
Army was a prisoner in his custody. It must
have been like a thunderbolt to Arnold, but his
self-control was such that he showed but slight
disturbance; he told the aides-de-camp that he
found he must go immediately to West Point,
and asked them to say to General Washington,
when he came, that he had been unexpectedly
called over the river and would soon return.

" He ordered a horse to be made ready, then
left the table and went upstairs to his wife.
He told her that he must flee for his life, and
might never see her again. She fainted, but not
venturing to call for assistance, or to delay his
flight, he gave a farewell kiss to their sleeping

baby, ran from the room, mounted a horse belonging to one of Washington's aides, and hastened toward the river—not by the winding
road that led to the Beverly Dock, but along a
by-way that led down a steep hill which is yet
called Arnold's Path. He got into his barge,
and told the six oarsmen to push out into the
middle of the stream and pull for Teller's Point,
promising them two gallons of rum if they
would row rapidly. He told them he was going
on board the *Vulture* with a flag of truce, and
was obliged to make all possible haste, as he
wanted to return in time to meet General
Washington at his quarters.

"When they passed Verplanck's Point he
showed a white handkerchief, which served as
a flag of truce to both Captain Livingston at
the Point and Captain Sutherland of the
Vulture—lying in sight a few miles below. No
one followed or tried to intercept them, and
they reached the *Vulture* without difficulty.
Arnold introduced himself to the captain, then
told his oarsmen that they were prisoners.
They answered indignantly that they had come
aboard under a flag of truce and had a right to

be allowed to go back free. Arnold coolly told them they must remain on board. Captain Sutherland did not interfere; but, despising Arnold's meanness, he gave the coxswain a parole to go on shore and get such things as he wanted, and when they arrived at New York Sir Henry Clinton set them all at liberty."

"Arnold was one mean wretch! I am sorry to have to own him as an American!" exclaimed Lucilla.

"Didn't the British despise him, papa?" asked Elsie.

"Yes, many of them did—regarding him with scorn as a reptile unworthy of that esteem which a high-souled traitor, a traitor because of great personal wrong, might claim.

"You remember Arnold had said when he left the breakfast table at the Robinson House that he was going to West Point. Shortly after his departure Washington came in. On being told that Arnold had gone across the river to West Point, he took a hasty breakfast, then said he would go over again and meet Arnold there. Hamilton did not go with the others, and it was arranged that the general and his suite should return and all take dinner there.

"As they were crossing the river Washington remarked that they would be greeted with a salute, as General Arnold was at the Point; but to their surprise all was silent when they drew near the landing. Colonel Lamb, the commanding officer, came strolling down a winding path, and was quite confused when he saw the barge touch the shore. He apologized to Washington for his seeming neglect of courtesy, saying that he was entirely ignorant of his intended visit. 'Sir, is not General Arnold here?' asked Washington in surprise.

"'No, sir,' replied Colonel Lamb, 'he has not been here these two days, nor have I heard from him within that time.'

"That aroused Washington's suspicions, but he went around examining the works at West Point, and about noon returned to the Beverly Dock, from which he had departed.

"As he was going up from the river to the house, Hamilton was seen coming toward the party with a hurried step and an anxious, troubled countenance. He said something to

Washington in a low tone; they went into the house together, and Hamilton laid before the chief several papers which furnished conclusive evidence of Arnold's guilt. They were the documents which Arnold had put in André's hands. With them was a letter from Colonel Jameson and one from André himself.

"Jameson, thinking Washington was still in Hartford, had sent a messenger there with these papers. While on the way the messenger heard of the return of Washington, and, hurrying back, took the nearest route to West Point through Lower Salem, where André was in custody. So he became the bearer of André's letter to Washington. He reached the Robinson House four hours after Arnold had left it, and placed the papers in Hamilton's hands.

"Washington called in Knox and Lafayette to give their counsel. He was calm, but full of grief. 'Whom can we trust now?' he said. As soon as the papers had been examined, Washington despatched Hamilton on horseback to Verplanck's Point, that an effort might be made there to stop the traitor.

"But it was too late; Arnold had got nearly

six hours the start of him. When Hamilton reached the Point a flag of truce was approaching from the *Vulture* to that post. The bearer brought a letter from Arnold to Washington. Hamilton forwarded it at once to the commander-in-chief, then wrote to Greene, who was at Tappan, advising him to take measures to prevent any attempt the British might make to carry out the traitor's plans.

"But the plot had failed; and when Sir Henry Clinton heard of it the next morning, on the arrival of the *Vulture* at New York, knowing that the Americans must now be wide awake to their danger, he gave up all thought of carrying out his scheme for getting possession of West Point."

The captain paused in his narrative, and Eric asked, "What did Arnold write to Washington about, uncle?"

"To ask protection for his wife and child, and to say that love for his country had actuated him in this thing."

"Humph! a queer kind of love I should say," sneered the boy.

"Yes; a love that led him to do all in his

power for the utter destruction of her liberties."

"And was Washington good to his wife and child?"

"Yes, very kind and sympathizing; and she was soon able to rejoin her husband—going down the river to New York with her babe.

"Washington promptly sent orders to General Greene to march with his portion of the army toward King's Ferry. Greene did not get the order before midnight, but by dawn his whole division was on the march. Washington sent a letter to Colonel Jameson also, telling him to send André to Robinson's house under a strong guard. That order also was received at midnight; André was aroused; and, though the night was very dark and rain falling fast, a guard under Major Tallmadge set off with the prisoner. They rode the rest of the night, and reached their destination at dawn of the 26th. On the evening of that day André was taken over to West Point, and on the morning of the 28th to Tappan. But we have already finished his story."

"I wish our folks could have got Arnold and punished him!" exclaimed Eric.

"Didn't they even try at all, uncle?"

"Yes, and came very near succeeding," said the captain. "You will find an interesting story about it in Lossing's 'Field Book of the Revolution.'"

"Oh, please tell it to us now!" cried several young voices; and the captain kindly complied.

"There was a very strong feeling of sympathy for André, both in the army and among the people outside of it," he said, "and, along with that, anger and disgust toward Arnold— the arch-traitor—and a strong desire to punish him as his wickedness deserved. There were various plans made to capture him—some of them secret, some open. It was while the army was still at Tappan that the one I just spoke of was undertaken. There were only three persons—Washington, Major Henry Lee, and Sergeant Champe—who knew of it.

"The idea was Washington's. He had learned that Arnold's quarters in New York were next door to those of Sir Henry Clinton, and that the traitor seemed to feel so safe that

he was not very cautious and watchful. Major
Henry Lee was the commandant of a brave
legion of cavalry, a man in whose prudence,
patriotism, and judgment Washington knew he
could confide; for he had already intrusted to
him the delicate service of ascertaining the
truth of flying rumors that other officers of
high rank were likely to follow Arnold's wicked
example.

"'I have sent for you, Major Lee,' Washington said to him, 'in the expectation that you
have in your corps individuals capable and willing to undertake an indispensable, delicate, and
hazardous project. Whoever comes forward on
this occasion will lay me under great obligations
personally, and in behalf of the United States
I will reward him amply. No time is to be
lost; he must proceed, if possible, to-night.'

"He then went on to explain what he
wanted, and Lee promptly replied that he had
no doubt his legion contained many men daring
enough to undertake any enterprise, however
perilous; but for the service required there was
needed a combination of talent rarely found in
the same individual. He then suggested a plan

which was highly approved by Washington. He said that Champe, the sergeant-major of his cavalry, was one very well qualified for the service, but he feared that his sense of personal honor would not allow him to take the first step in the perilous expedition,—desertion,—for he was anxiously awaiting a vacancy in the corps to receive a promised commission.

"John Champe was a Virginian, a native of Loudon County; he was twenty-three or twenty-four years of age; he had enlisted in 1776; he was a grave, thoughtful man and as unlikely as anyone to consent to do anything ignominious. Lee sent for him at once, told him what Washington wanted, and used all the eloquence of which he was master to persuade him to undertake the perilous work. Champe listened with the closest attention and evident excitement, and, when Lee had concluded, said that he was charmed with the plan and the proposed results; then went on to say that he was ready to attempt anything for his country's good, no matter how dangerous, that did not involve his honor; but the idea of desertion to the enemy and hypocritically espousing the king's cause

was an obstacle in his way too grave to be disregarded; so he must ask to be excused.

"Lee earnestly replied to these arguments;
told him that desertion at the request of his beloved commander, and for such reasons, carried
with it no dishonor; it was a laudable purpose;
success would bring him personal honor, and the
stain upon his character would last only till prudence would allow the publication of the facts.

"A great deal of persuasion was necessary,
but at last Lee succeeded; Champe consented
to undertake the perilous task, and they at once
set about the necessary preparations.

"Washington had his instructions already
drawn up. They were read to Champe, he taking note of them in such a way that no one else
could understand their true meaning. He was
to deliver letters to two persons in New York,
unknown to each other, but who had both been
long in Washington's confidence. He was to
procure such aid in bringing Arnold away as he
deemed best, but was strictly enjoined to for-
bear killing the traitor under any circumstances.

"All these matters having been settled, they

next considered the difficulties that lay in Champe's way between the camp and the enemy's outposts at Paulus Hook. There were many pickets and patrols in the way, and often parties of American irregulars in search of booty or adventure. Major Lee could not offer Champe any aid against these dangers lest he should be charged with favoring his desertion; so the sergeant was left to manage his flight as well as he could without help, Lee only doing what he could to delay pursuit as long as possible after it should become known that the sergeant-major had deserted.

"It was eleven o'clock at night when Champe took his orderly book, his cloak, and valise, and, with three guineas in his pocket,— given him by Lee,—mounted his horse secretly and started on his perilous expedition. Lee went at once to his bed, but not to sleep. He was doubtless much too anxious and excited for that. Within an hour the officer of the day, Captain Carnes, came hurrying in to tell him that one of the patrols had fallen in with a dragoon, who, on being challenged, put spurs to his horse and escaped.

"Lee was slow in replying; pretended to be very weary and drowsy—only half awake. In this way he detained the captain for some little time before he seemed fairly to understand what was wanted. Then he ridiculed the idea that one of his dragoons had deserted; for such a thing had occurred only once during the whole war.

"But the captain would not be convinced by any such arguments, and by Lee's reluctant orders immediately mustered a squadron of horse, satisfied himself and Lee that one had deserted, and that it was no less a personage than Champe, the sergeant-major, who had decamped with his arms, baggage, and orderly book.

"Captain Carnes ordered an immediate pursuit. Lee delayed the preparations as much as possible, and, when all was ready, ordered a change in the command, giving it to Lieutenant Middleton, a young man of so tender a disposition that he would no doubt treat Champe leniently should he catch him.

"Champe, however, was not caught. These delays had given him an hour's start of his pursuers. It was a bright starry night and past twelve o'clock when Middleton and his men mounted their horses and spurred after him.

"Lossing tells us that the horses of Lee's regiment were all shod by a farrier attached to the corps, and every shoe, alike in form, had a private mark put upon it; so the footprints of Champe's horse were easily recognized; for a fall of rain at sunset had effaced other tracks, and often before it was light enough to see them readily, a trooper would dismount and examine them. Ascending a hill near the village of Bergen, they saw from its summit their deserting sergeant not more than half a mile away. Champe saw them at the same moment, and both he and they spurred on as rapidly as possible. They were all well acquainted with the roads in that part of the country. There was a short cut through the woods to the bridge below Bergen. Middleton divided his party, sending a detachment by the short road to secure the bridge, while he and the others pursued Champe to Bergen. As Paulus Hook could not be reached without crossing the bridge, he now felt sure of capturing the deserter.

"The two divisions met at the bridge and were much astonished to find that nothing was to be seen of Champe. He knew of the short cut, thought his pursuers would take it, and therefore decided to give up the plan of joining the British at the Hook and take refuge on board of one of two of the king's galleys that were lying in the bay about a mile from Bergen.

"Middleton hurried from the bridge to Bergen, and asked if a dragoon had been seen there that morning. He was told that there had been one there, but nobody could say which way he went from the bridge. They could no longer see the print of his horse's shoes, and for a moment were at a standstill. But presently a trail was discovered leading to Bergen; they hurried on, and in a few moments caught sight of Champe near the water's edge, making signals to the British galley. He had his valise containing his clothes and his orderly book lashed to his back. When Middleton was within a few hundred yards of him he leaped from his horse, threw away the scabbard of his sword, and, with the naked blade in his hand, sped across the marsh, plunged into the deep waters of the bay, and called to the galley for help. In response to that a boat with strong oarsmen was quickly sent to his help, and directly he was in the galley with all the evidences of his desertion.

"Before night he was safely quartered in New York, having arrived there with a letter from the captain of the galley to Sir Henry Clinton in which the scene of his escape from the American troopers was described.

"Middleton's men picked up Champe's cloak and the scabbard of his sword, then caught his horse and returned with it to Tappan. As Lee caught sight of the articles he took them to be evidence that Champe had been killed, and was grieved at the thought; but his grief was turned into great joy when he learned from Middleton that the sergeant had escaped safely on board one of the enemy's galleys.

"Four days later a letter in a disguised hand, and without signature, came to Lee. It told of the occurrences of Champe's escape, and Lee knew it was from him.

"The British were much pleased with the desertion of Champe, as they knew that Lee's

legion was considered very faithful and that
therefore this desertion was an evidence of increasing defection among the American troops.
Champe did what he could to increase the idea
by adroit answers to questions asked of him,
giving the impression that he had a strong desire to serve the king. Clinton gave him a
couple of guineas, and advised him to call upon
Arnold, who was engaged in raising an American legion to be composed of loyalists and deserters. Arnold received him politely, gave him
quarters among his recruiting sergeants, and
invited him to join his legion. Champe begged
to be excused from that, saying that if caught
by the rebels he would surely be hanged; but
added that if he changed his mind he would
surely join his legion.

"Champe soon found means to deliver the
letters Washington had entrusted to him, made
arrangements with one of the correspondents
to aid him in his designs upon Arnold; then
communicated with Major Lee, telling him that
he had made inquiries in regard to those who
were suspected of beginning to favor the enemy,
and learned that there was no foundation for

the report. Soon he enlisted in the traitor's
legion that he might have free intercourse with
him and learn his night habits and pursuits.
He soon discovered that it was Arnold's custom
to return to his quarters about midnight and
then to visit a garden at the back of his house
which extended down to the edge of the river.
Adjoining the garden was a dark alley leading
to the street. All this seemed favorable to
Champe's design. He arranged with two ac-
complices a plan which seemed feasible: a boat
was to be in readiness on the river; they were to
seize and gag Arnold, carry him through the
alley, and from there through the most unfrequented streets to the river; and should anyone
attempt to interfere with them on the way they
were to represent him as a drunken soldier
whom they were taking to the guardhouse.
When once they had reached the boat there
would be no further difficulty.

" Champe was to remove some of the palings
in the garden fence and replace them so
slightly that they could be easily, quietly, and
quickly taken out when desired. When all was
arranged he wrote to Lee and appointed the

third subsequent night for the delivery of the
traitor on the Jersey shore.

"No doubt Lee was well pleased, and on that
evening he and a small party left the camp
with three accoutred horses—one for Arnold,
one for Champe, and one for the man who was
assisting him—and concealed themselves at a
place agreed upon in the woods at Hoboken.
There they remained hour after hour until
dawn, but no Champe and no prisoner appeared. They were much disappointed, but a
few days later Lee received a letter from
Champe telling how their plan had failed, and
assuring him that nothing could be done in the
matter at present.

"He said that on the very day when his plan
was to have been carried out Arnold changed
his quarters in order to superintend the em-
barkation of troops for an expedition southward
to be commanded by himself. In this expedition the legion in which Champe had enlisted
in order to carry out his plans was to take part,
and the poor fellow was in a sad dilemma. Instead of crossing the Hudson that night with
the traitor as his prisoner, he had been obliged

to go on board a transport with that traitor as his commander; and that to fight against, instead of for, his country."

"Oh, papa, did he go and fight against his country?" asked Elsie, drawing a long breath of surprise and sympathy.

"He had to allow himself to be carried to Virginia along with the troops of the enemy, and, I suppose, to go into battle with them," replied the captain; "but I dare say he was careful not to shoot any of the Americans. He watched his opportunity to desert, and after a time succeeded in so doing. He went up into the mountains of North Carolina, and when Lee and his legion were pursuing Lord Rawdon, he joined them. His old comrades were greatly astonished to see him—a deserter, as they supposed—and that Major Lee gave him a most cordial reception. But the truth was soon told, and then his old corps showed the greatest love and admiration for him. They were very proud of him, but he was discharged from service because it was very certain that the British, if they could get hold of him, would hang him."

"Is he alive now, papa?" asked Ned.

"Oh, no, my son; he died in 1798—a hundred years ago. At that time we were threatened with a war with France, and Washington, appointed to the chief command of our armies, sent to Colonel Lee to inquire for Champe, intending to make him a captain of infantry. But it was too late; the brave and gallant soldier had gone to another world."

"Dear man! I hope he went to heaven!" exclaimed Little Elsie in quivering tones.

"I hope so," responded her father.

There was a moment of silence, presently broken by Ned. "Papa, you know you promised to tell about Nathan Hale; please won't you do it now?"

"I will," replied the captain. "He was a fine, brave, good young man; described as very handsome—six feet tall, perfectly proportioned, light-blue eyes beaming with intelligence, roseate complexion, and soft light-brown hair. He was overflowing with good humor, and always ready to help anyone in distress. He received a good education, his father wishing him to enter the ministry; but he was teaching

school in New London when the news of the
Battle of Lexington came. A town meeting
was at once held, and Hale was one of the
speakers. He urged prompt action, saying,
' Let us march immediately, and never lay
down our arms until we have obtained our
independence.'

" He took part in the siege of Boston, and was
made a captain in January, 1776. He went to
New York and did good service there. Early
in the fall, in response to a call from General
Washington, he volunteered to enter the British
lines and procure intelligence. Disguised as a
schoolmaster and loyalist, he visited all of the
British camps on Long Island and in New
York, openly making observations, drawings,
and memoranda of fortifications. When he had
about finished his work, he was seized by the
British and taken before Sir William Howe.
On the evidence of papers found in his shoes,
he was condemned as a spy, and Sir William ordered him to be hanged. He asked for a Bible,
but it was refused him, nor would they let him
see a minister. He had written letters to his
sisters and to his betrothed, but his cruel cap-

tors destroyed them before his eyes. That last was done by William Cunningham—one of the most notoriously cruel Tories of the war. He afterward gave as his reason for that act of cruelty that he meant the rebels should never know they had a man who could die with such firmness.

"As Hale mounted the scaffold he said, 'You are shedding the blood of the innocent; if I had a thousand lives I would lay them down in the defence of my injured, bleeding country'; and his last words were, 'I only regret that I have but one life to lose for my country.'

"A country that may well remember him with love and pride," said Grandma Elsie.

"Oh, what wicked, wicked things they do in war times!" sighed Little Elsie.

"Yes," said her grandma; "war is itself a wicked thing: wholesale murder—sometimes on both sides, always on one."

"When the folks on one side are fighting for freedom, that's right, isn't it?" asked Eric.

"Yes; everyone not a criminal has a right to life, liberty, and the pursuit of happiness."

"Is it right to hang a man just for being a spy?" asked Ned.

"Not always, I'm sure," exclaimed Eric. "It wasn't right to hang Nathan Hale, I'm sure, for he was a good man, and only doing what he could to save his country."

"Very true," said his father; "and he is now one whose memory is cherished and honored, while that of Cunningham—his cruel executioner—is abhorred."

"I'd rather be entirely forgotten than remembered as a cruel, wicked wretch!" exclaimed Eric.

"Yes; as any right-minded person would," said his father.

CHAPTER VIII.

SHORTLY after breakfast the next morning the whole party were on the yacht, and it was speeding down the river. West Point was their first halting-place. Some hours were spent there; they were just in time for the battery drill; after that they climbed to the top of Mount Independence, enjoyed the view, and visited the ruins of " Old Fort Put "; came down, and then went back to their yacht, promising themselves another and longer visit to West Point some days later.

The captain pointed out the sites of forts Montgomery and Clinton as they passed, and told of their building by the Americans during the War of the Revolution and their destruction by the British in 1777.

" As Lossing tells us," said Captain Raymond, " ' They fell beneath one heavy blow suddenly and artfully dealt by a British force from New York, and the smitten garrison were scattered like frightened sheep upon the mountains.' "

" Oh, papa, surely they didn't surrender without fighting at all? " exclaimed Lulu.

" No indeed, daughter; they fought long and desperately. General James Clinton and his brother George were their commanders. As I have told you before, I think, General Clinton established his headquarters at a place called Washington Square, about four miles west of the village of New Windsor, and there collected his dispersed troops preparatory to marching to the relief of Kingston, then threatened by the enemy."

" But they didn't get there in time to save it from being burned by the British," said Edward Leland. " What dreadful times those were! "

" Yes," said Grandma Elsie; " we may be very thankful that we live in these better days. And in the best and freest country in the world; which it wouldn't have been, if God had not been for us in those days of trial."

It was a pleasant morning, and all sat under an awning on the deck, preferring it as the breeziest spot and affording the best view of the beautiful country on either side with its many historical associations. Captain Raymond drew attention to Verplanck's and Stony points as they passed them.

"Yonder is Verplanck's Point," he said; "and there, overlooking the river, stood, in Revolutionary times, Fort Fayette; and yonder, on the other side, is Stony Point, where was another small fort. They were captured by Sir Henry Clinton on the 1st of June, 1779. The garrison of Stony Point consisted of only forty men, and that at Verplanck's of seventy, commanded by Captain Armstrong. The British flotilla was commanded by Admiral Collier. The troops landed in two divisions on the morning of May 31—the one, under Vaughan, on the east side eight miles below Verplanck's; the other, under Clinton, on the west side a little above Haverstraw. There was no fight at Stony Point, as the garrison retired to the Highlands, knowing that the forces of the enemy were too overwhelming to be successfully resisted. The British took possession; dragged up cannon and mortars during the night;

pointed them and the guns found in the fortress
toward Fort Fayette, and in the morning began
a heavy cannonade upon it. At the same time
the fort was attacked in the rear by Vaughan
and his troops, and the little garrison surrendered themselves prisoners of war.

" The loss of these forts was a grief to Washington, and he determined to make an effort to
recover them, for their loss endangered West
Point. He soon ordered an attack upon them
by the Americans under the command of Generals Wayne and Howe. Wayne had his quarters at Sandy Beach, fourteen miles from Stony
Point, and on the morning of July 15 all the
Massachusetts light infantry was marched to
that place. It was an exceedingly sultry day,
and the march—begun at noon, taking them
through narrow defiles, over rough crags, and
across deep morasses—must have been hard indeed; they moved in single file and at eight in
the evening rendezvoused a mile and a half below Stony Point. They rested there while
Wayne and several other officers reconnoitred
the enemy's works. Then they formed into
column, and moved silently forward under the

guidance of a negro slave belonging to a Captain Lamb living in the neighborhood."

" New York was a slave State at that time? " exclaimed Sydney inquiringly.

" Yes," replied Captain Raymond; " England had forced slavery upon her Colonies here, and it was not yet abolished. Captain Lamb was a warm Whig, and Pompey seems to have been one also. Soon after the British took possession of the fort, he ventured to carry strawberries there for sale; the men of the garrison were glad to get them, and Pompey became quite a favorite with the officers, who had no suspicion that he was regularly reporting everything to his master.

" At length Pompey told them that his master would not allow him to come with his fruit in the daytime, because it was now hoeing-corn season. The officers, unwilling to lose their supply of luxuries, then gave him their countersign regularly so that he could pass the sentries in the evening. He had it on the night of the attack, and gave it to the Americans, who used it as their watchword when they scaled the ramparts. It was ' The fort's our own.' "

" And they could say it with truth," laughed Lucilla; " for the fort was really theirs—stolen from them by the British."

" The fortress seemed almost impregnable," resumed her father; " built upon a huge rocky bluff, an island at high water, and always inaccessible dryshod,—except across a narrow causeway in the rear,—it was strongly defended by outworks and a double row of abatis. There was a deep and dangerous morass on one side, and on the other three were the waters of the Hudson."

" And was the rock too high and steep to climb, papa? " asked Ned.

" Yes, indeed! But our men were brave and persevering fellows; Wayne, their leader, believed in the old saying ' Where there's a will there's a way.' He practiced upon that, and in consequence was very successful. He was so rapid and earnest in what he did that people took to calling him ' Mad Anthony Wayne.'

" Now, he resolved to storm this fort at all hazards, as Lossing says, and only waited for the ebbing of the tide and the deep first slumber of the garrison.

" At half-past eleven o'clock that night the Americans began a silent march toward the fort. Two strong men disguised as farmers, and the negro Pompey, went first: There was no barking of dogs to arouse the garrison, for they had all been killed—all in that neighborhood—the day before. Pompey gave the countersign to the first sentinel on the high ground west of the morass, then the two disguised men suddenly seized and gagged him. The same thing was done with the sentinel at the causeway. Then, as soon as the tide ebbed sufficiently, the greater part of Wayne's little army crossed the morass at the foot of the western declivity of the promontory, no one among the enemy observing them. Three hundred men under General Muhlenburg remained as a reserve in the rear. The troops were divided into two columns—all with unloaded muskets and fixed bayonets. At a little past midnight the advance parties moved silently to the charge, one on the northern and the other on the southern part of the height. The two main divisions followed them, one led by Wayne himself. The Americans were not discovered by the British

until they were within pistol shot of the pickets
on the heights, when a skirmish took place between the advance guards and the sentinels.

"The Americans used only their bayonets,
as they had been ordered, but the pickets fired
several shots; and those sounds of strife waked
the garrison, and the silence of the night was
broken by the loud cry 'To arms! to arms!'
the roll of the drum, the rattle of musketry
from the ramparts and the abatis, and the roar
of the cannon, charged with deadly grapeshot,
from the embrasures. It was a terrible storm,
but our brave fellows forced their way
through it—through every obstacle—until the
vans of all the columns met in the centre of the
works, where they arrived at the same time.
Each of our men had a white paper in his hat
which, as it could be seen in the dim light, enabled him to distinguish friend from foe."

"I think Wayne was wounded in the fight,
wasn't he?" asked Mr. Leland.

"Yes," replied the captain; "at the inner
abatis he was struck on the head by a musket
ball, the blow causing him to fall to his knees.

His aides, Fishbow and Archer, raised him to his feet and carried him gallantly through the works.   He believed himself mortally wounded, and exclaimed as he arose, ' March on, carry me into the fort, for I will die at the head of my column! '   But, fortunately, he was not so badly wounded as he supposed, and was able to join in the loud huzzas which arose when the two victorious columns met within the fort.

"The garrison surrendered as prisoners of war, and I am glad and proud to say were treated with clemency by the victors. Not a life was taken after the flag was struck and quarter asked for."

"Was anybody killed before that, papa? " asked Little Elsie in anxious tones.

"Yes, daughter," he replied; "15 Americans lost their lives and 83 were wounded; 63 of the British were killed and their commander and 543 officers and men taken prisoners. Down in the river below were some British vessels. They slipped their cables and moved down to a place of security.

"So prompt was Wayne that he did not wait

for daylight to send in his report to Washington. 'Dear General: The fort and garrison with Colonel Johnson are ours. Our officers and men behaved like men who are determined to be free,' was what he wrote."

"Oh, I like that! It reminds me of Perry's despatch to Harrison after his victory on Lake Erie," exclaimed Lucilla.

"Did our people get back the other fort, uncle?" asked Eric.

"No; the guns of the Stony Point fort were turned upon it at dawn the next morning and a desultory firing kept up during the day, but delays and misunderstandings prevented an intended attack from being made in time to dislodge the garrison; Sir Henry Clinton getting news of their danger in time to send them help.

"Washington saw that we could not retain Stony Point, because he could not spare enough troops to hold it; so he ordered the stores and ordnance to be removed, the fortress to be evacuated, and the works destroyed; all of which was accordingly done on the night of the 18th."

"And did the British find out what was going on and attack our fellows?" asked Eric.

"Yes; the heavy ordnance was placed upon a galley to be conveyed to West Point; but as soon as it moved a cannonade began from Verplanck's and the British shipping near by. A heavy shot from the *Vulture* struck the galley below water mark, and she went down near Caldwell's Landing. The British again took possession of Stony Point, but little of value was left them there except the eligible site for a fortification."

"Wayne was very much praised for the taking of Stony Point, wasn't he, papa?" asked Grace.

"Yes; the storming and capture of Stony Point was esteemed one of the most brilliant exploits of the war,—an exhibition of skill and indomitable courage,—and General Wayne, the leader of the enterprise, was everywhere greeted with rapturous applause. Congress gave him a vote of thanks. It also resolved that a gold medal, emblematic of that action, be struck and presented to General Wayne. Also, rewards were given to the other officers and to the men."

"Papa, wasn't the home of Captain Molly somewhere in this neighborhood?" asked Grace.

"Yes; Lossing tells us that she lived, at the close of the war, between Fort Montgomery and Buttermilk Falls, and was generally dressed in a woman's petticoats with an artilleryman's coat over them—perhaps an old one of her husband's, for he was a cannonier. They were both in Fort Clinton when it was taken by the British. When the Americans retreated and the British scaled the ramparts, her husband dropped his match and fled. Molly picked it up, touched off the piece, then scampered after him and the others. As you probably remember, she was again with her husband in the Battle of Monmouth, and when he was shot down took his place at the cannon and worked it through the rest of the engagement. For that act of bravery Washington rewarded her with a sergeant's commission."

"I think she deserved it," said Grace. "I admire her bravery, but I don't know what would tempt me to go into a battle."

"I should be sorry indeed to have you go into

one," returned her father, regarding her with a fond smile.

The yacht was now moving rapidly down the river, all on board greatly enjoying the beautiful scenery. They landed at Tarrytown and visited the historical spots in its vicinity, among them the scene of André's capture and the monument to his captors.

"Why did they name this place Tarrytown, uncle?" asked Eric.

"Probably from the fact that a great deal of wheat was raised in the vicinity. 'Tarwe Town'—meaning wheat town—was what the early Dutch settlers called it.

"Those living here in Revolutionary days saw stormy scenes. There were lawless bands of marauders called Cowboys and Skinners infesting the Neutral Ground, which extended for thirty miles along the river and was plundered by both bands of outlaws without much, if any, regard to their victims' loyalty or disloyalty to the country."

"Those were bad times to live in," remarked Little Elsie. "I'd a great deal rather live in these; though I should like to have seen Washington and Wayne and Lafayette and—oh, all the rest of the good, brave men who did so much to save our country! "

" Yes," said Grandma Elsie, " but though we cannot see them here, we may hope to meet at least some of them in another and a better world."

CHAPTER IX.

A PLEASANT surprise awaited our party on their return to Crag Cottage that evening, the bride and groom—Rosie and her husband—having arrived during their absence. Everybody was glad to see them; and, with the accommodations of the yacht to supplement those of the house, there was room and to spare.

Finding such to be the case, and that it was very pleasant to be together, all remained Evelyn's guests for another week, in which a great deal of time was passed upon the river taking repeated views of beautiful historic scenes.

But at length they separated for a time—some remaining where they were; some going to the seashore; while Grandma Elsie and the Raymonds, leaving the yacht at New York City, crossed the mountains into Pennsylvania, visited some historical scenes in that State, then traveled on through Ohio from south to north-spent a few weeks among the islands of Lake Erie; then, the yacht having come to them again by the northern route, returned home in it by way of the Welland Canal, the St. Lawrence River, and the Atlantic Ocean. On their route through Pennsylvania they spent a few days at Pocono, visiting the points of interest about there. Wilkesbarre was their next stopping place, for they all wanted to see the beautiful Valley of Wyoming.

"Is Wyoming an English name?" asked Elsie Raymond, as they drove through the valley.

"No," said her father; "it comes from the language of the Delawares, and means 'large plains.' It is probable that the Delawares were the first tribe which lived there."

"And is Wilkesbarre an Indian name too?" she asked.

"No; it is a compound of the names of two Englishmen who were good friends to America in the times of the Revolution—John Wilkes and Colonel Barre.

"The first European to visit the valley was Count Zinzendorf," continued the captain.

"He was of an ancient Austrian family. He was a Christian man and very earnest in trying to do good. He travelled through Germany, Denmark, and England, and in 1741 came to America and preached at Bethlehem and Germantown. He was very desirous to do the poor Indians good, so travelled about among them, though he had no companions except an interpreter. In one of these excursions he crossed the Pocono, and came into this Valley of Wyoming. At this time he had with him a missionary named Mack and his wife. They pitched their tent upon the western bank of the Susquehanna, at the foot of a high hill and near a place in the river known as Toby's Eddy.

"Not very far away was a Shawnee village. The Indians held a council there to hear what these missionaries had to say, but could not believe that they had come all the way across the Atlantic just to teach religious truth to them. The conclusion they came to was that these strangers had come to spy out their country and rob them of their lands. Thinking thus, they made up their minds to murder the count. But they feared the English, there-

fore instructed those appointed to do the deed
to be very secret about it.

"On a cool September night two stout Indians went stealthily from the town to the missionary's temporary dwelling—a tent with a
blanket hung across the doorway. They drew
the blanket stealthily aside and peeped in.
They made no noise, and he was not aware of
their presence, as he reclined on a bundle of
weeds engaged in writing or in devout medita-
tion.

"As Lossing says: 'The benignity of his
countenance filled them with awe, but an incident (strikingly providential), more than his
appearance, changed the current of their feelings. The tent cloth was suspended from the
branches of a huge sycamore in such a manner
that the hollow trunk of the tree was within its
folds. At its foot the count had built a fire,
the warmth of which had aroused a rattlesnake
in its den; and at the moment when the savages
looked into the tent the venomous reptile was
gliding harmlessly across the legs of their intended victim, who did not see either the ser-
pent or the lurking murderers. At that sight

they at once entirely changed their opinion of him and regarded him as under the special protection of the Great Spirit.' They were filled with profound reverence for him, and went back to their tribe with such an account of his holiness that their enmity was changed to veneration."

"And I think history says a successful mission was established there," remarked Grandma Elsie, as the captain paused, as if at the end of his story.

"Yes," he replied, "and it was continued until a war between the Shawnees and the Delawares destroyed the peace of the valley."

"What was that war about, papa?" asked Ned.

"Like many others it was about a very foolish thing," replied the captain. "The Shawnees were a not very powerful tribe, and lived by permission of the Delawares on the western bank of the Susquehanna. One day the warriors of both tribes were hunting upon the mountains when a party of women and children of the Shawnees crossed to the Delaware side to gather fruit, and were joined by some of the Delaware squaws and children. After a while two of the children—a Shawnee and a Delaware—got into a quarrel over a grasshopper. Then the mothers took part,—the Shawnees on one side, the Delawares on the other,—and the Delawares, who were the more numerous, drove the Shawnees home, killing several on the way. When the Shawnee hunters came home, saw their dead women, and heard the sad story, they were very angry, crossed the river, and attacked the Delawares. A bloody battle followed; the Shawnees were beaten, and retreated to the banks of the Ohio, where lived a larger portion of their tribe."

" There are not many more historic scenes in this State that we will care to visit at this time, are there, papa?" asked Grace.

" I think not," he said; " we are going west, and most of them are already east of us."

" But, father," said Lucilla, " we have hardly touched upon the history of Wyoming."

" True," he returned; " but it is so very sad that I fear its recital would rather detract from the enjoyment of this lovely scenery. How-

ever, I will give you a brief account of what
took place here during the Revolutionary War.

"Early in the summer of 1778 the movements of Brant and his warriors, the Johnsons
and Butlers and their Tory legions, upon the
upper waters of the Susquehanna, and the
actions of the Toriès in the Wyoming Valley,
greatly alarmed the people. Nearly all their
able-bodied men were away in the Continental
Army; none was left to defend the valley but
old men, boys, and women. Afraid of the savages, they were building six forts, going through
all the labor required in that work without
payment except the hope of self-defence.

"Such was their condition when in June,
1778, an expedition of Tories and Indians was
ready to come down upon them. All this was
told to Congress. Wyoming men in the army
besought protection for their wives and little
ones, and General Schuyler wrote a touching
letter in their behalf. But all Congress did
was to pass resolutions to let the people
take measures for self-defence by raising troops
among themselves, and finding their own arms,
accoutrements, and blankets.

"The people—poor creatures!—did their best; but, attacked by overwhelming numbers of the most savage foes, they went through tertible scenes and sufferings. I will not dwell further upon the horrors of that dreadful time. The Tories and Indians acted like fiends. Lossing, speaking of what occurred after the fight and surrender, says: ' The terms of capitulation were respected by the invaders, particularly the Indians, for a few hours only. Before night they spread through the valley, plundering and burning.' "

" Did the women and children run away, papa? " asked Ned.

" Yes; they fled to the mountains, and many of them perished in the Pocono Mountain swamp, known as the Shades of Death, and along the wilderness paths by the way of the Wind Gap and Water Gap. They were flying to the settlements on the Lehigh and Delaware. They were not travelling like ourselves—in an easy carriage, with abundance of food and clothing; and many died from hunger and exhaustion."

" Some of their clothes had been taken by the

Indians," remarked Violet. "I remember reading that many squaws had on from four to six dresses of silk or chintz, one over the other; and some four or five bonnets, one over another."

"Papa, are we going to visit any more places in this State where they had fights?" asked Ned.

"Where there were battles fought, son? No, I think not at this time. We will probably go on into Ohio now without any more delays."

"There were some fights there—weren't there, papa?" asked Elsie.

"Yes; between the whites and the Indians, and between the Americans and the British and Indians, in the war of 1812--14."

"Yes, children," said Lucilla; "don't you remember papa's telling us about some of the fights near Lake Erie, and Perry's victory on the lake?"

"Oh, yes!" exclaimed both the little ones; "and his letter to General Harrison—'We have met the enemy and they are ours.' And you'll tell us about the land fights, won't you, papa?"

"Yes," he said; "one of these days; probably while we are in Ohio."

"Are we going right on now to the islands in Lake Erie, papa?" asked Grace.

"Unless some one or more of us should desire to stop by the way," returned the captain pleasantly.

"Perhaps it would be more restful to pass a night at Pittsburg or Cincinnati," suggested Grandma Elsie; and that was what was decided upon, after a little discussion of the question.

They rested in Cleveland for another night; then, on a bright morning, passed over to the islands in a steamer. A pleasant surprise awaited them on landing; their cousin Ronald Lilburn was there with his wife Annis and her grandnephew, Percy Landreth. The last-named was one whom Captain Raymond would have preferred not to have in the company,— but merely on Lucilla's account,—and he greeted him with cordial kindness.

"We have given you a surprise, haven't we?" asked Mrs. Lilburn of her cousin Elsie.

"Yes; a most pleasant one," replied Mrs.

Travilla. " I can truly say I think your presence here will double our enjoyment. How
long since you arrived? "

" Only about twenty-four hours. We came
straight from home, where we left all your
dear ones well."

" Ah, that is good news! It is a new thing
for me to be so far away from my dear father;
and he is growing old; so I have been feeling a
little anxious about him."

" He evidently misses you, but is glad that
you are enjoying yourself," said Annis.

" Yes! so unselfish as he is—my dear father!
Ah, how lovely it is here! " glancing about as
she spoke. " No doubt we can pass some days
or weeks here very delightfully."

" I am quite sure of it, mother," said the captain, who had overheard the remark, made as
they all were on their way from the landing to
the hotel. " We will have the yacht here in a
day or two, I think; and it will afford us some
pleasant trips here and there on the lake."

" And carry us to some historical scenes,
won't it, papa? " asked Grace in a tone of satisfaction.

"Yes," he replied; "and we will live on it, unless the majority of our company should prefer the hotel."

"No danger of that, I think," said Grandma Elsie; "we all feel so much at home and find ourselves so comfortable on the yacht."

"I don't wonder that you prefer it," said Annis; "but I was hoping you would all be at the hotel with us."

"Are you not willing to be on the *Dolphin* with us?" asked the captain, giving her a cordial look and smile.

"Indeed, sir, I should like nothing better— except for the fear of crowding you."

"I think that is beyond your ability," laughed the captain. "Even joined by all three of you, we should have more room than we have had in some of our trips which we found very enjoyable."

"Then we accept your kind invitation with the greatest pleasure," said Mr. Lilburn; and there the conversation ended, as they were already at the entrance to the hotel.

They spent a pleasant day in and about there, but early in the evening the *Dolphin* made her appearance, and they all went aboard of her— a blithe and happy company.

The morning found them all in good health and good spirits, and as they sat about the breakfast table the captain asked: " Where shall we go to-day? I think it would be well to take the little trips we contemplate while the weather is so favorable. Then when a storm comes we can shut ourselves in and enjoy books, work, and each other's company."

" I think that is a good suggestion, captain," said Grandma Elsie. " Suppose you take us to-day to Fremont, to view the ground where Fort Stephenson stood."

Everyone present seemed pleased with the proposition, and it was decided to make the little excursion that morning. They could go nearly all the way in their yacht, by lake and river, and shortly after breakfast found themselves in motion—the *Dolphin* having lain quietly at anchor during the night.

" I, for one, should like to refresh my memory in regard to Fort Stephenson: when it was built, by whom attacked, and how defended," remarked Annis, as they sat together on the deck while sailing toward Sandusky Bay. "Captain Raymond, you are usually the story teller, I believe."

"Ah, Cousin Annis, that is a fine character you give me," he returned with a smile. "But perhaps I deserve it. Do all the company feel the same desire that Mrs. Lilburn has just expressed?"

"I do," said Grandma Elsie; "and from the expression of the faces of the others present I am quite sure that they do also."

"Yes, indeed, papa; I am sure we do!" cried Lucilla and Grace in a breath, Percy Landreth, Elsie, and Ned joining eagerly in the request; and the captain at once began.

"Fort Stephenson was built in 1812; the garrison consisted of 160 men under the command of Major George Croghan, then but twenty-one years of age. It was on the 31st of July, 1813, that it was invested by a large force of British and Indians under the command of Proctor. The fort was not a strong one; its chief defences were three block houses, circumvallating pickets from fourteen to sixteen feet high, and a ditch about eight feet wide and as many feet deep; they had one iron six-pounder cannon. Of course, swords and rifles were not lacking, and the men were Kentucky sharpshooters.

" General Harrison heard that the British were moving against Fort Stephenson. He had visited the fort, and felt convinced that it could not be held against an attack with heavy artillery, so had said to Major Croghan: ' Should the British approach you in force with cannon, and you can discover them in time to effect a retreat, you will do so immediately, destroying all the public stores. You must be aware that to attempt a retreat in the face of an Indian force would be vain. Against such an enemy your garrison would be safe, however great the number.'

" On learning of the intended descent of the British upon Fort Stephenson, Harrison held a consultation with his officers—McArthur, Holmes, Graham, Paul, Hukill, Wood, and Ball. They were unanimously of the opinion that Fort Stephenson could not be successfully defended against an enemy approaching in such force, and that Major Croghan ought imme-

diately to comply with his general's standing
order to evacuate."

"Moving order, I should think, father,"
laughed Lucilla.

"Yes," returned the captain with a smile;
"but knowing Croghan's innate bravery, Harrison feared he would not move promptly, so sent
him another order to abandon the fort. It was
carried by a white man named Connor and two
Indians. They started at midnight and lost
their way in the dark. So they did not reach
the fort until the next day about eleven o'clock,
and by that time the woods were swarming with
Indians.

"Major Croghan called his officers together
and consulted them in regard to a retreat. A
majority were of his opinion—that such a step
would be disastrous, now that the Indians
swarmed in the woods, and that the post might
be maintained.

"Croghan immediately sent a reply to Harrison's order, saying it had come too late to be
carried into execution, that they had determined to maintain the place—that they could
and would do so. It was a disobedience of

orders, but not so intended. The gallant young major thought that the previous order, which spoke of the danger of a retreat in the face of an Indian force, justified him in remaining, as that force was already there when this second order reached him.

"But the general considered it disobedience, which could not be permitted. He at once sent Colonel Wells to Fort Stephenson to supersede Croghan, and ordered Croghan to headquarters at Seneca Town. Colonel Wells was escorted by Colonel Ball with his corps of dragoons. On the way they were attacked by about twenty Indians, and quite a severe skirmish ensued. Seventeen of the Indians were killed."

"Papa, did Major Croghan go to the general? and was he very cross to him?" asked Ned.

"He went promptly, made a full and satisfactory explanation to General Harrison, and was directed to go back to his command the next morning; which he did, feeling more than ever determined to maintain his post in spite of British and Indians. General Harrison kept scouts out in all directions to watch the movements of the enemy. On the evening of Saturday, the 31st of July, one of those parties, lingering on the shore of Sandusky Bay, about twenty miles from Fort Stephenson, saw that Proctor was approaching by water. They made haste to return to headquarters with their information, stopping on the way at Fort Stephenson and making it known there.

" Croghan was watchful, wide awake to the dangers that surrounded them. A good many Indians had been seen upon the high ground on the eastern side of the Sandusky River, but had scampered away on being fired at from the six-pounder in the fort.

" At four o'clock in the afternoon the British gunboats, bringing Proctor and his men, were seen at a turn in the river more than a mile distant. They were greeted by shots from the six-pounder, but they came on; and at a cove somewhat nearer the fort, opposite a small island in the stream, they landed with a five-and-a-half-inch howitzer.

" At the same time the Indians showed themselves in the woods on all sides. In this attacking force there were four hundred British

and several hundred Indians. And Tecumseh
was stationed upon the roads leading from
Fort Meigs and Seneca Town with almost two
thousand more. These were intended to intercept any re-enforcements that might be coming
to Croghan's assistance. Having thus, as he
thought, cut off Croghan's retreat, Proctor
sent Colonel Elliott and Captain Chambers to
demand the instant surrender of the fort. With
them was Captain Dixon of the Royal
Engineers, who was in command of the
Indians.

"They came with a flag of truce, and Croghan sent out Second-Lieutenant Shipp, as his
representative, to meet the flag.

"The usual salutations were exchanged, then
Colonel Elliott said, 'I am instructed to demand the instant surrender of the fort, to spare
the effusion of blood, which we cannot do
should we be under the necessity of reducing
it by our powerful force of regulars, Indians,
and artillery.'

"'My commandant and the garrison,' replied Shipp, 'are determined to defend the post
to the last extremity, and bury themselves in its

ruins rather than surrender it to any force whatever.'

" ' Look at our immense body of Indians,' interposed Dixon. ' They cannot be restrained from massacring the whole garrison, in the event of our undoubted success.'

" ' Our success is certain,' eagerly added Chambers.

" ' It is a great pity,' said Dixon, in a beseeching tone, ' that so fine a young man as you and as your commander is represented to be, should fall into the hands of the savages. Sir, for God's sake surrender, and prevent the dreadful massacre that will be caused by your resistance! '

" ' When the fort shall be taken there will be none to massacre,' Shipp coolly replied, for it was not long since, at Fort Meigs, he had had dealings with the same foe. ' It will not be given up while a man shall be able to resist.'

" He was just turning to go back to the fort, when an Indian sprang from a bushy ravine near at hand and tried to snatch his sword from him. The indignant Shipp was about to despatch the Indian, when Dixon interfered.

Then Croghan, who was standing on the ram‹
parts watching the conference, called out,
'Shipp, come in, and we'll blow them all
to ——!' At that, Shipp hurried into the fort,
the flag was returned, and the British immediately opened fire from their gunboat and the
five-and-a-half-inch howitzer which they had
landed, beginning the attack before proper
arrangements could be made.

" It seems the Indians had had an alarm and
let the British know of it. A Mr. Aaron North,
knowing nothing of the proximity of British
or Indians, was riding through the wood, drawing near the fort on the other side of the Sandusky, when he discovered a large body of Indians scattered along the river bank and half
concealed by the bushes. He wheeled his
horse and fled in the direction of Seneca. The
startled Indians fired several shots after him,
but without hitting him. The Indians doubtless told the British of all this, and Proctor
thought the horseman a messenger to Harrison
to inform him of the attack upon Fort Stephenson, and that the result would probably be
that re-enforcements would be sent to Croghan,

would beat back Tecumseh, and fall upon him at Sandusky.

" All night long the five six-pounders which had been landed from the British gunboats, and the howitzer, played upon the stockade without doing any serious damage. Occasionally the besieged answered with their one cannon, which they moved from one blockhouse to another, to give the impression that the garrison had several heavy guns. But their supply of ammunition was small, and Croghan was too wise to waste it. He determined not to use any more in firing at random in the dark; so ordered Captain Hunter, his second in command, to place it in the blockhouse at the middle of the north side of the fort, so as to rake the ditch in the direction of the northwest angle—the point where the enemy would be most likely to make the assault, because it was the weakest part.

" That was done before daylight, and the gun, loaded with a half-charge of powder and a double charge of slugs and grapeshot, was completely masked.

" During the night the British had dragged

three of their six-pounders to a place in the woods where the ground was higher than the fort and about 250 yards from it. Early in the morning they began a brisk fire upon the blockade from those and the howitzer."

"Oh, papa, how dreadful!" exclaimed Elsie. "Did all of our men get shot?"

"No; the cannonade produced very little effect, and Proctor grew very impatient. The long hot day was nearly done, and the Indians were becoming restless. At four o'clock in the afternoon he ordered all his guns to fire upon that weak northwest angle.

"Then Croghan and his men set to work to strengthen it as much as possible. They piled bags of sand and sacks of flour against the pickets there, which materially broke the force of the cannonade. At five o'clock a dark thunder cloud was seen in the west and the thunder seemed like the echo of the enemy's cannon. Then the British came on in two close columns, led by Brevet Lieutenant-Colonel Short and Lieutenant Gordon. At the same time a party of grenadiers, about 200 strong, under Lieutenant-Colonel Warburton, took a wide circuit

through the woods to make a feigned attack
upon the southern front of the fort, where Captain Hunter and his party were stationed.

"There was in the fort at the time a man
named Brown, a private of the Petersburgh
volunteers, with a half-dozen of his corps and
Pittsburgh Blues. To them was entrusted the
management of the six-pounder in the fort, for
Brown was skilled in gunnery.

"The British artillery played incessantly
upon the northwestern angle of the fort, causing a dense smoke, and under cover of that a
storming party under Lieutenant-Colonel Short
advanced to within fifteen or twenty paces of
the outworks before they were discovered by the
garrison. But they were Kentucky sharpshooters, and every man of them was at his post.
Instantly they poured upon the assailants a
shower of rifle balls sent with such deadly aim
that the British were thrown into confusion.
But they quickly rallied. The axemen pushed
bravely forward over the glacis, and leaped into
the ditch to assail the pickets. Short was at
their head, and when a sufficient number were
in the ditch behind him, he shouted, 'Cut away

the pickets, my brave boys, and show the d——d Yankees no quarter!'

"Now the time had come for the six-pounder to make itself heard. The masked port flew open instantly, and the gun spoke with terrible effect. Slug and grapeshot streamed along that ditch overflowing with human life, and spread awful havoc there. Few of those British soldiers escaped. The second column of the storming party made a similar attempt, but was met by another discharge from the six-pounder and another destructive volley of rifle-balls."

"Was anybody killed, papa?" asked Ned.

"Yes, a good many were," replied his father. "Colonel Short, Lieutenant Gordon, Laussaussie of the Indian Department, and 25 privates were left dead in the ditch, and 26 of the wounded were made prisoners. Three other officers were slightly wounded, but escaped. The rest of the attacking party retreated in haste and disorder.

"It was not until after that disaster that Warburton and his grenadiers reached the south front of the fort. When they did, Hunter's corps assailed them with a destructive volley, and they fled for shelter to the adjacent woods. It is said that Lieutenant-Colonel Short, when he fell, twisted a white handkerchief on the end of his sword, asking the mercy he had exhorted his men not to show to the Americans."

"Oh, I hope they did show it to him, papa," said Elsie.

"I think they would have done so had opportunity offered," said the captain; "but he was found dead in the ditch."

"And were any of our people killed?" she asked.

"One man was killed and 7 were slightly wounded; while, according to the most careful estimates, the loss of the British in killed and wounded was 120. They behaved most gallantly, getting no assistance from the cowardly Indians, who kept themselves out of harm's way in a ravine near by.

"The assault had lasted only about half an hour. Lossing tells us, 'The dark storm cloud in the west passed northward, the setting sun beamed out with peculiar splendor, a gentle breeze from the southwest bore the smoke of

battle far away over the forest toward Lake
Erie, and in the lovely twilight of that memorable Sabbath evening the brave young
Croghan addressed his gallant little band with
eloquent words of praise and grateful thanks-
giving. As the night and the silence deepened,
and the groans of the wounded in the ditch fell
upon their ears, his generous heart beat with
sympathy. Buckets filled with water were let
down by ropes from the outside of the pickets;
and as the gates of the fort could not be opened
with safety during the night, he made a communication with the ditch by means of a
trench, through which the wounded were borne
into the fort and their necessities supplied.' "

"Oh, how good and kind he was!" exclaimed
Grace. "I am proud of him as one of my
countrymen. Is he still living, papa?"

"No, daughter; he died in New Orleans on
January 8, 1849."

"The anniversary of the great victory there
in the War of 1812! Was he not rewarded for
his gallant defence of Fort Stephenson?"

"Yes; he was brevetted lieutenant-colonel
for his gallantry, and some twenty years later

Congress voted him a gold medal in acknowledgment of it. In 1846 he joined Taylor's
army in Mexico and served with credit at the
Battle of Monterey."

" You have given us an interesting tale, captain," remarked Cousin Ronald as the story
seemed to have come to an end—" one that was
really new to me; for I have read but little
about that war—which I hope we can always
refer to as the last between the mother country
and this, my adopted one—the native land of
my bonny young wife," he added with a loving
and admiring look at Annis.

" Ah, my dear, how true it is that love is
blind," said Annis softly, giving him a look of
fond appreciation.

" Ha, ha! A pair of old lovers! " laughed a
voice that seemed to come from somewhere in
the rear of the little party.

" Yes, that's what we are," said Annis with
mirthful look and tone.

" And who are you that dares to say such
saucy things to our company? " asked Ned,
looking sharply round toward the spot from
which the voice had seemed to come.

"Somebody that has a tongue of his own and a right to use it," returned the voice, but the speaker was still invisible.

"Well, whoever you are you've no business here on my father's yacht without an invitation," cried Ned, hurrying toward the spot from which the strange voice seemed to come.

"You silly, impudent youngster! I'm not here without an invitation," said the voice, seeming to come from a greater distance than before.

"Not?" exclaimed Ned; "then who invited you?"

"The captain and owner of the vessel."

Ned turned to his father. "Did you invite him, papa, and who is he?" Then, perceiving a look of amusement on every face, "Oh, I know! Why didn't I think before? It's just Cousin Ronald playing he's somebody else."

"Yes, laddie, and he's rather an auld mon to be playing at anything," returned the old gentleman pleasantly. "Dinna ye think so?"

"No, sir; and it's good of you to make a little fun for us youngsters."

"As well as for us older folks," added his mother in a sprightly tone.

"I thought it was a fellow who had no business here," said Ned, "but you are as welcome as anything, Cousin Ronald."

"Aye, laddie, I dinna doubt it or I wadna be here," laughed the old gentleman; "but I know there are no more hospitable folk to be found anywhere then these American cousins o' mine."

"I should think not, sir," said Neddie with a smiling glance from one parent to the other; "and I believe there's nobody they like better to entertain than you."

"Is Fort Stephenson still standing, papa?" asked Grace.

"No," was the reply, "but we can see the site, which is in the bosom of the village of Fremont, and covers about two-thirds of a square. We will no doubt find someone who can and will point it out to us and show us the ravine where the Indians fled after the first discharge of the rifle-balls by the garrison; and the iron six-pounder cannon that did such great execution in defence of the fort; also the landing place of the British.   By the way, the garrison named that cannon the 'Good Bess.'"

"Oh, I hope we will see it," said Ned.   "I'd like to."

They reached their destination in time to see the cannon and all the interesting places and things made memorable by their connection with the struggle at Fort Stephenson, then returned to the yacht, sailed out into the bay again, and anchored for the night.

CHAPTER X.

THE next morning Lucilla woke early—as was usual with her—and presently joined her father upon the deck. He greeted her, as was his custom, with a smile and a tender caress, asking if she were quite well and had passed a comfortable night.

"Yes, papa," she said; "I slept as soundly as possible, and feel perfectly well this morning; as I hope you do."

"I do, for I also enjoyed a good night's rest and sleep."

The yacht was moving, and Lucilla remarked it with some surprise.

"I thought we were lying at anchor," she said.

"So we were through the night," replied her father, "but now we are travelling toward Fort Meigs—or perhaps I should rather say its ruins."

"Oh, that will be an interesting spot to visit!" exclaimed Lucilla. "Just where is it, papa?"

"On the Maumee River, opposite Maumee City, situated at the head of river navigation, eight miles from Toledo."

"Wasn't it somewhere in that region that Wayne fought one or more of his battles with the Indians?"

"Yes; he took possession of and fortified the place where St. Clair was defeated, and called it Fort Recovery. That was in 1794. On the 30th of June he was attacked by about a thousand Indians with some British soldiers and Canadian volunteers, who assailed the garrison several times. Fifty-seven Americans were killed, wounded, and missing; also 221 horses. The Indians said they lost more than in their battle with St. Clair.

"A few weeks later Wayne was joined by Major-General Scott with 1600 mounted volunteers from Kentucky, and two days later he moved forward with his whole force toward the Maumee. Remembering the sad fate of St. Clair and his men, Wayne moved very cautiously; so slowly and stealthily that the Indians called him the 'Black Snake.' He had faithful, competent scouts and guides, and he moved by unfrequented ways, with perplexing feints. Twenty-five miles beyond Fort Recovery he built Fort Adams. Again he moved forward for four days, then encamped on a beautiful plain at the confluence of the Maumee and Auglaize rivers, on the site of the present town of Defiance; I presume from the fort Wayne built there, and which he called Fort Defiance. He found there a deserted Indian town with at least a thousand acres of corn growing around it. Wayne was now in full possession of power to subjugate and destroy the Indians, but, unwilling to shed blood unnecessarily, he sent them a message with kind words. 'Be no longer deceived or led astray by false promises and language of bad white men at the foot of the rapids; they have neither the power nor the inclination to protect you.'

"He offered them peace and tranquillity, and invited them to send deputies to meet him in council without delay.

"But they rejected his overtures, and said in reply, 'Stay where you are for ten days, and we will treat with you; but if you advance we will give you battle.'

"Wayne was, however, too wise and wary to be deceived by them. He saw that nothing but a severe blow would break the spirit of the tribes and end the war, and, as Lossing says, he resolved to inflict it mercilessly.

"On the 15th of August his legion moved forward, and on the 18th took post at the head of the rapids, near the present town of Waterville, where they established a magazine of supplies and baggage, protected by military works, and named it Fort Deposit. There, on the 19th, Wayne called a council of war and adopted a plan of march and battle proposed by Lieutenant Harrison."

"Afterward general, papa?"

"Yes, nineteen years later he had become general-in-chief, and performed gallant exploits in this same valley of the Maumee.

"The next morning after that council, at eight o'clock, Wayne advanced according to that plan. They had gone forward about five miles when the advance corps, under Major Price, was terribly smitten by heavy volleys from the concealed foe and compelled to fall back. The enemy was full 2000 strong—composed of Indians and Canadian volunteers, and they were arranged in three lines within supporting distance of each other.

"Wayne's legion was immediately formed in two lines, principally in a dense wood on the borders of a wet prairie, where a large number of trees had been prostrated by a tornado, which made the movements of cavalry very difficult, besides affording a fine covert for the enemy. But Wayne's troops fell upon them with fearful energy, soon making them flee, like a herd of frightened deer, toward Fort Miami."

"The fort the British had built upon our ground without so much as saying by your leave?"

"The very same. They reached it by a hasty flight of two miles through the thick woods, leaving forty of their number dead on the way, by the side of each of whom lay a musket and bayonet from British armories.

"Three days and three nights Wayne and his army remained below the rapids, making such desolation as seemed necessary for the subjugation of the hostile Indians and the treacherous Britains and Canadians; all that in defiance of the threats of the commandant of Fort Miami, though his guns were within view of the American tents. He—Colonel McKee—was the chief instigator of the war with the Indians, with whom he was carrying on a most lucrative trade, and he had there extensive storehouses and dwellings. These our troops set fire to and destroyed, as they did all the products of the fields and gardens."

"That seems a pity, papa, but I suppose it was necessary."

"Yes; as no doubt those British men well knew. Wayne's men sometimes were within pistol-shot of Fort Miami, but its guns kept silence. The commander did a good deal of scolding and threatening; Wayne coolly defied him and retorted with vigor. But neither went any farther.

"Wayne and his troops remained there until the middle of September, when they went to the head of the Maumee; and at the bend of the river, just below the confluence of the St. Mary's and St. Joseph's, which form it, they built a strong fortification and called it Fort Wayne. By the latter part of October it was finished and garrisoned with infantry and artillery, under Colonel Hamtramck.

" The rest of the troops then left, some for Fort Washington, to be discharged from the service, and others for Fort Greenville, where Wayne made his headquarters for the winter. There the various tribes with whom he had been at war came to him—by deputations—and agreed upon preliminary terms of peace. They remembered that he had assured them that the British had neither the power nor the inclination to help them—and how that assurance had been verified by the silence of the guns of Fort Miami.

" They promised to meet him in council early the next summer, and did so. Early in June chiefs and sachems began to reach Fort Greenville, and on the 16th of that month a grand council was opened there. Almost 1100 Indians were present, and the council continued until the 10th of August. On the 3d of that month a satisfactory treaty was signed by all parties. And by a special treaty between the United States and Great Britain the western military posts were soon evacuated by the

British, and for fifteen years the most remote frontier settlements were safe from any annoyance by the Indians."

"And that encouraged emigration to the Northwestern Territory, did it not, papa?" asked Lucilla.

"Yes," he said, "and in consequence the country grew rapidly in population of a hardy kind."

"Until the War of 1812."

"Yes; and it was in that war that Harrison did so much to distinguish himself as a patriot and a brave and skilful officer."

"And it was then he built the Fort Meigs you are taking us to, papa?"

"Yes; at the Maumee Rapids in February, 1813. It was named for Return Jonathan Meigs, who was then Governor of Ohio."

"Return Jonathan! what an odd name!"

"Yes, and there is an odd story connected with it. Years before the Revolution a bright-eyed coquette was courted by Jonathan Meigs. On one occasion he pressed his suit with great earnestness and asked for a positive answer. She would not give it, but feigned coolness, and he—growing discouraged—resolved to be trifled with no longer, so bade her farewell forever. He took his departure, but had not gone far down the lane when she ran after him and at the gate called out, ' Return Jonathan; return Jonathan!'

"He did go back to her; they afterward married, and were very happy together; and when the first son was born they named him Return Jonathan.

"He was born in 1740; was the heroic Colonel Meigs who did such valiant service in the Revolutionary War, and was one of the early settlers of Ohio, going there in 1788. His son Return Jonathan was elected Governor of Ohio in 1810 and held that office until 1814.

" Harrison arrived at Fort Meigs on the 12th of April, 1813, and was glad to find there 200 Pennsylvanians, patriotic men, who, though anxious to go home to put in their spring seeds, assured him that they would never leave him until he thought their services could be spared without danger to the cause. He discharged them on the arrival of three Kentucky companies.

"While on his way Harrison had been told of frequent appearances of Indian scouts in the neighborhood of the rapids, and of little skirmishes with what he supposed to be the advance of a more powerful foe. That alarmed him, and he despatched a messenger to Governor Shelby of Kentucky asking him to send to the Maumee the whole of the 3000 men who had been drafted in that State. He brought with him about 300 men in all, but was agreeably surprised to find, on his arrival, that there were no signs of the enemy being near in great force.

"But that enemy was at that very time preparing to strike a destructive blow at Fort Meigs. Tecumseh was even then at Fort Malden with almost 1500 Indians. Proctor had fired his zeal and that of his brother, who was called the Prophet, by promises of future success in their schemes for confederating the tribes, and boasting of his ample power to place Fort Meigs with its garrison and immense stores in the hands of his Indian allies.

"Proctor was delighted with this response of the savages to his call, and had fine visions of the victory he was going to gain, and the glory and promotion it would bring him. He was more boastful than ever, and treated the Americans at Detroit in a supercilious manner. He ordered the Canadians to assemble at Sandwich on the 7th of April and told them the campaign would be short, decisive, successful, and profitable."

"How did he know!" exclaimed Lucilla scornfully.

"He did not," said her father; "events shortly following showed it to have been but idle boasting. That boast was made on the 7th of April. On the 23d his army and his savage allies embarked on a brig and several smaller vessels, accompanied by two gunboats and some artillery. On the 26th they were at the mouth of the Maumee, about twelve miles below Fort Meigs, and two days later they landed on the left bank of the river near old Fort Miami, and established their main camp there.

"Captain Hamilton of the Ohio troops was reconnoitring down the river with a small force on the 28th, when he discovered the enemy there in force. They were first seen by Peter

Navarre, one of Harrison's most trusty scouts. Hamilton sent him in haste to Fort Meigs with the news, and Harrison at once despatched him with three letters—one for Governor Meigs at Urbana, one for Upper Sandusky, and one for Lower Sandusky. Fort Meigs was quite strong —had intrenchments, pickets, several block-houses, and a good supply of field-pieces; but from the account he had had of the character and strength of the enemy, Harrison considered it in imminent peril. He knew that General Clay was on his march with his Kentuckians, and immediately after despatching Navarre with his letters, he sent Captain William Oliver, the commissary of the fort, and a brave, judicious, and intelligent officer, with a verbal message to Clay urging him to press forward by forced marches.

" Oliver found General Clay at Defiance with 1200 Kentuckians. At St. Mary's blockhouse Clay divided his brigade. He descended the St. Mary himself with Colonel Boswell's corps, while Dudley went down the Auglaize.

" The two divisions were to meet at Defiance. But before Dudley had reached that point he heard of Harrison's perilous position at Fort Meigs. A council of officers was called, and it was resolved to send Harrison word that succor was at hand. It was a very dangerous errand and required someone who was well acquainted with the country. Leslie Combs, a brave, patriotic young man, whom Clay had commissioned captain of a company of riflemen as spies or scouts, volunteered to go.

" ' When we reach Fort Defiance,' he said, ' if you will furnish me a good canoe, I will carry your despatches to General Harrison, and return with his orders. I shall only require four or five volunteers from my own company.' His offer was joyfully accepted by Dudley. The next morning, May 1, they reached Defiance, and as soon as a canoe could be procured, Combs and his companions—Paxton, Johnson, and two brothers named Walker—started on their perilous errand. They had with them also a Shawnee warrior named Black Fish. He took the helm, the other four the oars, while Combs was at the bow in charge of the rifles and ammunition.

" As they pushed off from Fort Defiance

there were cheers and sad adieus, for few thought they would ever see them again. It was a dangerous voyage; rain was falling fast and the night was intensely dark. Combs was determined to reach Fort Meigs before daylight the next morning. They passed the rapids in safety, but not till quite late in the morning, and then heard heavy cannonading in the direction of the fort. That told them that the siege had begun, which made an attempt to reach the fort far more perilous than it would otherwise have been.

"Combs had now a hard choice to make. It would be prudent to go back, but would not seem courageous, while to stay where they were till the next night, or to go on at once, seemed equally hazardous. But he was very brave and soon came to a decision. 'We must go on, boys,' he said; 'and if you expect the honor of taking coffee with General Harrison this morning, you must work hard for it.'

"He knew the weakness of the garrison and feared it could not hold out long. Therefore great was his joy when, on sweeping round Turkey Point, at the last bend in the river, he saw the Stripes and Stars waving over the be-leaguered camp. His little company evinced their delight by a suppressed shout. That was a sad mistake, for, suddenly, a solitary Indian appeared in the edge of the woods, and in another moment a large body of them could be seen in the gray shadows of the forest, running eagerly to a point below to cut off Combs and his party from the fort.

" He attempted to dart by them, when a volley of bullets wounded Paxton and Johnson—the latter mortally. The fire was returned with effect, then the Shawnee turned the prow to the opposite shore, and the voyagers left the canoe and fled toward Defiance. They tried to take Johnson and Paxton with them, but found it impossible, so were compelled to leave them to become captives.

" At the end of two days and two nights Combs and Black Fish reached Defiance, where they found Clay and his troops just arrived. The Walkers were there also, having fled more swiftly than Combs and the Indian had been able to because of their efforts to aid the flight of the two wounded men. They had suffered terribly in their flight, and for a time Combs was unable to take command of his company, but he went down the river with the re-enforcements and took an active part in the fight at Fort Meigs.

"But, ah, here come others of our party, and I must leave the rest of my story to be told later in the day," added the captain, turning to greet Violet and his younger children, who at that moment appeared upon the deck.

CHAPTER XI.

SHORTLY after breakfast, when the whole of their little company had gathered beneath the awning upon the deck, the captain resumed his story, as all had expressed a desire to hear it.

"On the morning of the 30th of April, 1813," he said, "the British had completed two batteries nearly opposite Fort Meigs and mounted their ordnance. On one there were two twenty-four pounders, on the other three howitzers. Well-directed round-shot from the fort had struck some of their men while at work, but neither that nor the drenching rain stopped them.

"Harrison had been busy too. He addressed his soldiers eloquently in a general order.

"'Can the citizens of a free country, who have taken arms to defend its rights,' he said, 'think of submitting to an army composed of mercenary soldiers, reluctant Canadians goaded to the field by the bayonet, and of wretched, naked savages? Can the breast of an American soldier, when he casts his eye to the opposite shore, the scene of his country's triumphs over the same foe, be influenced by any other feeling than the hope of glory? Is not this army composed of the same materials as that which fought and conquered under the immortal Wayne? Yes, fellow soldiers, your general sees your countenances beam with the same fire that he witnessed on that glorious occasion; and although it would be the height of presumption to compare himself with that hero, he boasts of being that hero's pupil. To your posts then, fellow citizens, and remember that the eyes of your country are upon you.'

"That general order was given on the morning that the British made their appearance, and when he saw that they were erecting batteries on the opposite shore that would command his works, he directed his men to make a traverse, or wall of earth, on the highest ground through the middle of his camp. It had a base of twenty feet, was three hundred yards long and twelve feet high. While they were at the work it was concealed by the tents, which when it was finished were suddenly removed to its rear.

"Then the British engineer perceived, to his great mortification, that his labor had been almost in vain. Instead of an exposed camp from which Proctor had boasted that he would soon smoke out the Yankees,—meaning quickly destroy it with shot and shell,—he saw only an immense shield of earth which hid the Americans and thoroughly sheltered them.

"Proctor then changed his plans somewhat and sent a considerable force of white men under Captain Muir, and Indians under Tecumseh, to the eastern side of the river, under cover of the gunboats, to attack the fort in the rear.

"The British batteries were silent through the night, but a gunboat, towed up the river near the fort under cover of darkness, fired thirty shots. The only effect, however, was an increase of the vigilance of the Americans. The next morning, though it was raining heavily, the British opened a severe cannonade and bombardment upon Fort Meigs, which they continued with slight intermissions for) about five days; but without doing much injury to the fort or garrison.

" Occasionally our men returned the fire by eighteen-pounders. But their supply of shot for these and the twelve-pounders was very small, and as they did not know how long the siege might last, it was thought best to use them very sparingly.

" The British seemed to have powder, balls, and shells in great abundance, and they poured a perfect storm of missiles—not less than five hundred—upon the fort the first day and until eleven o'clock at night."

" And was nobody hurt, papa? " asked Elsie.

" One or two of the garrison were killed," replied her father, " and Major Stoddard of the First Regiment, a soldier of the Revolution, was so badly wounded by a shell that he died ten days later of lockjaw.

" The British were building a third battery on the other side of the river; they finished it that night, and all the next day kept up a brisk cannonade.

" Within the next twenty-four hours a fourth

battery was opened. The British had been making mounds in the thickets near the angles of the fort, and that night a detachment of artillerists and engineers crossed the river and mounted guns and mortars upon them. One was a mortar battery, the other a three-gun gun battery. The Americans had expected something of the kind, and had raised traverses in time to foil their enemy; and when toward noon of the 3d the three cannon and the howitzers suddenly began firing upon the rear angles of the fort, they did scarcely any damage.

"A few shots by our men from their eighteen-pounders soon silenced the gun battery, and the British hastily moved the cannon and placed them near the ravine. During the 3d they hurled shot and shell steadily upon the fort, but with so little effect that the besiegers grew discouraged, and on the 4th the fire was not nearly so constant.

"Then Proctor sent Major Chambers with a demand for the surrender of the fort, and Harrison promptly responded, 'Tell General Proctor that if he shall take the fort it will be under curcumstances that will do him more honor than a thousand surrenders.'

" The cannonade from the fort was feeble because of the scarcity of ammunition, but the guns were admirably managed, and did good execution at every discharge. Captain Wood wrote, ' With plenty of it we should have blown John Bull from the Miami.'

" The Americans showed their ability to keep their foe at bay by frequently mounting the ramparts, swinging their hats, and shouting defiance at their besiegers. They were well supplied with food and water and could afford to spend time and weary their assailants by merely defensive warfare.

" Still Harrison was anxious, thinking how strong were the foe, and how Hull and Winchester had failed and suffered; he was looking hourly and anxiously up the Maumee for the hoped-for re-enforcements. Since Navarre and Oliver went out he had heard nothing from those whom he had expected to come to his aid. But near midnight on the 4th, Captain Oliver, Major Trimble, and 15 men who had come down the river in a boat, made their way into the fort, bringing the glad tidings that General Clay and 1100 Kentuckians would probably reach the post before morning, being but eighteen miles distant.

"The cannonading at Fort Meigs was distinctly heard at Fort Winchester, where Oliver had found Clay on the 3d, and Clay was hastening as fast as possible to Harrison's aid, moving down the river in eighteen flat scows, with sides furnished with shields against the bullets of the Indians who might be infesting the shores of the river.

"The head of the rapids was eighteen miles from Fort Meigs; it was late in the evening when the flotilla arrived there; the moon had gone down, and the sky was overcast with clouds, making a night so intensely dark that the pilot refused to go on before daylight. Trimble and the 15 others then immediately offered their services to go with Oliver to cheer Harrison and his men with the news that re-enforcements were almost at hand.

"It was joyful news to them. Harrison at once despatched Captain Hamilton and a subaltern in a canoe with an order to Clay bidding him detach about 800 men from his brigade and land them at a point about a mile or a mile and a half above Fort Meigs. The detachment was then to be conducted to the British batteries on the left bank of the river. These batteries were to be taken, the cannon spiked, and carriages cut down. The troops must then return to the boats and cross over to the fort.

"The rest of his men were to land on the fort side of the river, opposite the first landing, and fight their way into the fort through the Indians. Harrison knew that the British force at the batteries was not large, the main body being still near the old Fort Miami, and that the bulk of the Indians with Tecumseh were on the eastern side of the river. His object was to strike effective blows on both sides of the stream at the same time.

" While these orders of his were being carried out, he intended to make a sally from the fort, destroy the batteries in the rear, and disperse or capture the whole British force on that side of the river.

" Clay came down the river early the next morning, and about five miles above the fort

Hamilton met him with Harrison's order. Clay then directed Dudley to take the twelve front boats and carry out Harrison's commands in regard to the British batteries, while he should hasten forward and perform the part assigned to him.

"Colonel Dudley landed his detachment in fine order, and they gained the plain on which Maumee City now stands, unseen by the enemy, formed for marching in three parallel columns, one led by Dudley, one by Major Shelby, the other by Acting-Major Morrison. Captain Combs with 30 riflemen, including 7 friendly Indians, flanked in front fully a hundred yards distant. Thus they moved through the woods a mile and a half toward the British batteries, which were still firing upon Fort Meigs.

"There was a prospect of capturing the whole force, but Dudley had unfortunately failed to inform his men of his exact plans, and that was a fatal mistake. Shelby's column, according to his orders, moved on to a point between the British batteries and their camp below, when the right column, led by Dudley in person, raised the horrid Indian yell, rushed forward, charged with vehemence upon the enemy, captured the heavy guns, and spiked eleven of them without losing a man.

" At the same time the riflemen had been attacked by the Indians, and, not having been told that they were to fall back upon the main body, thought it their duty to fight. That was a fatal mistake, as the main object of the expedition was already fully accomplished, although the batteries were not destroyed. The British flag was pulled down, and as it reached the earth loud huzzahs went up from Fort Meigs. Harrison, who was watching from his chief battery, with intense interest, now signaled Dudley to fall back to the boats and cross the river according to his former orders.

" Probably Dudley did not see it, but he did see the Indians in ambush attacking Combs and his riflemen, and with a quick and generous impulse ordered them to be re-enforced. In response to that a great part of the right and centre columns rushed into the woods in considerable disorder, their colonel with them. It did not matter much at first, for, though they were undisciplined and disorderly, they soon

put the Indians to flight, thus relieving Combs
and his men; but, forgetting prudence, they
pursued the flying savages almost to the British
camp.

"When they started on that pursuit Shelby's
men still had possession of the batteries, but
the British artillerists, largely re-enforced, soon
returned and recaptured them, taking some of
the Kentuckians prisoners and driving the
others toward their boats. The Indians, too,
were re-enforced, came back, and fiercely attacked Dudley and his men, who were in such
utter confusion that it was impossible to command them. Shelby had rallied those that
were left of his column and marched them to
Dudley's aid; but they only participated in the
confusion and flight. That became a precipi-
tate and disorderly rout, and the greater part of
Dudley's command were killed or captured.
Dudley himself was overtaken, tomahawked, and
scalped. Of the 800 who followed him from
the boats, only 170 escaped to Fort Meigs.
Captain Combs and his spies were among those
who were taken and marched to Fort Miami
as prisoners of war."

"Oh, how dreadful it all was!" sighed **Grace.**
"I hope the other two parties had better success."

"Yes," her father said; "while what I have just been telling you was taking place on the left bank of the river, General Clay had tried to land the six remaining boats under his command nearly opposite the spot where Dudley had debarked with his; but the current, swollen by the heavy rains, was very swift, and drove five of them ashore. The sixth, in which were General Clay and Captain Peter Dudley, with fifty men, separated from the rest, kept the stream, and finally landed on the eastern bank of the river opposite to Hollister's Island. There they were fired upon by round-shot from the batteries opposite and by a crowd of Indians on the left flank of the fort.

"Clay and his party returned the attack of the Indians with spirit, and reached the fort without the loss of a man.

"Colonel Boswell's command landed near Turkey Point. The same Indians who fired upon Clay and his men now attacked these. Boswell and his men marched boldly over the low plain, fought the savages on the slopes and brow of the high plateau most gallantly, and reached the fort without much loss. He was greeted with shouts of applause and tharks, and met by a sallying party coming out to join him in a prompt attack upon that portion of the enemy whom he had just been fighting. There was only a moment's delay. Then they went out, fell upon the savages furiously, drove them half a mile into the woods at the point of the bayonet, and utterly routed them. So zealous were the victors that they would in all probability have made the same mistake that poor Dudley did, had not Harrison, watching them through a spyglass, on one of his batteries, and seeing a body of British and Indians gliding swiftly along the borders of the wood, sent an aide to recall them. He—the aide—was a gallant young fellow, and though he had a horse shot under him, he succeeded in communicating the general's orders in time to enable the detachment to return without much loss.

"Now General Harrison ordered a sortie from the fort against the enemy's works on the right, near the deep ravine. Three hundred and fifty men were engaged in that, and behaved with the greatest bravery. Lossing says, ' They charged with the fiercest impetuosity upon the motley foe, 850 strong, drove them from their batteries at the point of the bayonet, spiked their guns, and scattered them in confusion in the woods beyond the ravine toward the site of the present village of Perrysburg.' It was a desperate fight, and Miller lost several of his brave men. At one time Sebree's company were surrounded by four times their number of Indians, and their destruction seemed inevitable. But Gwynne of the Nineteenth, seeing their peril, rushed to their rescue with a part of Elliot's company, and they were saved. The victors returned to the fort, having accomplished their object, and bringing with them 43 prisoners. They were followed by the enemy, who had rallied in considerable force. After that day's fighting, the siege of Fort Meigs was virtually abandoned by Proctor. He was much disheartened, and his Indian allies deserted him; the Canadian militia did likewise."

"Was Tecumseh one of the deserters, papa?" asked Lucilla.

"No; but probably it was only his commission and pay as a brigadier in the British Army that kept him from being one. He had hated General Harrison intensely since the battle of Tippecanoe, in 1811, and was to have had him at this time as his peculiar trophy. He had been promised that, and the territory of Michigan had been promised his brother, the Prophet, as a reward for his services in the capture of Fort Meigs.

"Beside all these discouraging things, news came to Proctor that Fort George, on the Niagara frontier, was in the hands of the Americans and that the little army of Fort Meigs was soon to be re-enforced from Ohio. He saw nothing before him but the capture or dispersion of his troops should he remain, therefore he resolved to flee. But, to conceal that intention, and in order that he might move off with safety, he again sent a demand for the surrender of the fort.

"Harrison regarded it as an intended insult, and requested that it should not be repeated. Proctor attempted to take away with him his unharmed cannon, but a few shots from Fort

Meigs caused him to desist and go without them. One of his gunboats, in return, fired, killing several of our men. Among them was Lieutenant Robert Walker, of the Pittsburgh Blues, who was buried within the fort, and his grave may still be seen there, marked by a plain, rough stone with a simple inscription— 'Lieutenant Walker, May 9, 1813.'

"Papa, did the British carry off those of our men they had taken prisoners?" asked Elsie.

"Yes; and allowed the savages to rob, ill-treat, and butcher them in the most horrible manner. At Fort Miami they shot, toma-hawked and scalped more than 20, besides having murdered and plundered many on the way.

"It was Tecumseh who at last stopped the fiendish work, though not till after more than 40 had fallen. And this horrible work was done in the presence of General Proctor, Colonel Elliot, and other officers, as well as the British guard. They made them run the gauntlet for a distance of forty or fifty feet, killing or maiming them as they went, with pistols, war-clubs, scalping knives, and toma-hawks. In that way nearly, if not quite, as many were slaughtered as were killed in battle. When those who still remained alive had got within the fort, the savages raised the war-whoop, and began reloading their guns with the evident intention of resuming their horrid onslaught on the defenceless prisoners, when Tecumseh, being told of what was going on, hurried to the fort as fast as his horse could carry him. 'Where is General Proctor?' he demanded; then seeing him near, he asked why he had not put a stop to the massacre. 'Your Indians cannot be commanded,' replied Proctor, trembling with fear at the rage he saw in the chief's countenance. 'Begone!' retorted Tecumseh in disdain. 'You are not fit to command; go and put on petticoats.'"

"Was Proctor pleased with that answer, papa?" asked Ned, with a look of amusement.

"I think not greatly," replied the captain. "Tecumseh was much disappointed over their failure to take Fort Meigs, and urged Proctor to try again. Proctor did not feel willing, but at length, near the end of June, he consented, and they began making arrangements to do so.

"About that time a Frenchman who had been taken prisoner with Dudley's men escaped from the British, fled to Fort Meigs, and told Clay of the threatened danger. Clay at once sent word to Harrison, who was at Franklinton, and to Governor Meigs, at Chillicothe.

"Harrison believed it was the weaker posts of Lower Sandusky, Erie, or Cleveland, rather than Fort Meigs, they intended to attack. He ordered troops under Colonel Anderson, then at Upper Sandusky, to go at once to Lower Sandusky; also Major Croghan, with a part of the Seventeenth, and Colonel Ball with his squadron of cavalry. He had just held an important council with the Shawnee, Wyandot, Delaware, and Seneca Indians at his headquarters at Franklinton. Circumstances had made him doubt their fidelity, and he required them to take a determined stand for or against the Americans; to remove their families into the interior, or the warriors must go with him in the ensuing campaign and fight for the United States.

"Their spokesman assured the general of their unflinching friendship, and that the war-

riors were anxious to take part in the campaign.
Then Harrison told them he would let them
know what he wanted of them. ' But,' he said,
' you must conform to our mode of warfare.
You are not to kill defenceless prisoners, old
men, women, or children. By your good conduct I shall be able to tell whether the British
can restrain their Indians when they wish to
do so.'

" Then he told them of Proctor's promise to
deliver him into the hands of Tecumseh, and
added jestingly, ' Now if I can succeed in taking Proctor, you shall have him for your prisoner, provided you will treat him as a squaw, and
only put petticoats upon him, for he must be
a coward who would kill a defenceless prisoner.'

" Harrison followed Colonel Anderson and
his regiment, and, learning from scouts that
numerous Indians were seen on the lower
Maumee, he selected 300 men to make a forced
march to Fort Meigs. He arrived there himself on the 28th, and sent Colonel Johnson to
make a reconnoisance toward the Raisin to procure intelligence. Johnson went, and brought
back word that there was no immediate danger

of the enemy coming against Fort Meigs in force. Satisfied of that, Harrison left Fort Meigs to attend to duty at other points.

"That was on the 1st of July. Late in that month the British had fully 2500 Indians collected on the banks of the Detroit. These, with the motley force he had already there, made an army of fully 5000 men. Early in July bands of Indians had begun to appear in the vicinity of Fort Meigs, seizing every opportunity for killing and plundering. Tecumseh had become very restless and impatient; wanting to go on the warpath,—especially when he saw so many of his countrymen ready for it,— and he demanded that another attempt should be made to capture Fort Meigs. He made a plan for the attack, and proposed it to Proctor.

"It was that the Indians should be landed several miles below the fort, march through the woods to the road leading from the Maumee to Lower Sandusky, in the rear of Fort Meigs, and there engage in a sham fight. That, he thought, would give the troops in the fort the idea that re-enforcements were coming to them and had been attacked. Then the garrison would sally forth to aid their friends, and would at once be attacked in their turn by Indians lying in ambush, while the other Indians would rush into the fort and take possession before the gates could be closed.

"Proctor consented, thinking it a good plan. On the 20th of July he and Tecumseh appeared with their 5000 men at the mouth of the Maumee. General Clay sent a messenger to Harrison with that news. Harrison was doubtful whether it was Fort Meigs or Fort Stephenson they meant to attack, so removed his quarters to Seneca Town, from which he could co-operate with either. There he commenced fortifying his camp, and was soon joined by 450 United States troops and several officers, while another detachment was approaching with 500 regulars from Fort Massac on the Ohio River.

"On the afternoon of the 25th of July Tecumseh and Proctor tried their plan. The British concealed themselves in the ravine just below Fort Meigs; the Indians took their station on the Sandusky road; and at sunset they began their sham fight. It was so spirited, and accompanied by such terrific yells, that the garrison thought their commander-in-chief must be coming with re-enforcements and that he was attacked by the Indians; and they were very anxious to go out to his aid.

"But Clay was too wise to be taken in. A messenger who had just returned from a second errand to Harrison had had hairbreadth escapes from the Indians swarming in the woods; therefore, though Clay could not account for the firing, he felt certain that no Americans were taking part in the fight. Officers of high rank demanded permission to lead their men to the aid of their friends, and the troops seemed almost ready to mutiny because they were not permitted to go. But Clay remained firm; and well it was for them that he did.

"A few cannon shot were hurled from the fort in the direction of the supposed fight, and a heavy shower of rain came up. That put an end to the fighting, and all was as quiet as usual about Fort Meigs that night.

"Tecumseh's stratagem had failed, and as he and Proctor were ignorant of the strength of the garrison, they thought it best not to try an assault. They lingered in the neighborhood for some thirty hours, then withdrew to the old encampment near Fort Miami; and soon afterward the British embarked with their stores, and sailed for Sandusky Bay with the intention of attacking Fort Stephenson.

" The Indians were to assist in the attack, and a large number marched across the country for that purpose.

" Clay quickly despatched a messenger to Harrison with all this information. But I have already told you of the attack upon Fort Stephenson, and of its brave defence.

" Yes, papa; and it was very interesting," said Elsie. " Have we far to go now to get to Fort Meigs? and is it just as it was when Harrison and his men were there? "

" We may hope to get there soon," replied the captain; " as it is only eight miles above Toledo, and we are nearing that place now. But we shall find only ruins."

" Oh, papa, what a pity! " exclaimed Ned.

" Not a very great pity, I think," said his father. " It is not needed now, and I hope will not be ever again."

"I hope that famous elm tree is there yet," remarked Grandma Elsie.

"I do not know," replied the captain. "But probably it is."

"Oh, what about it, papa?" asked Elsie; and her father answered, "At the beginning of the siege all the water the garrison needed had to be taken from the river. The elm tree was on the opposite side of the river, and the Indians used to climb up and hide themselves in its thick foliage and from there fire across at the water carriers. In that way they killed several of our men. Then the Kentucky riflemen fired at them; and it is said that not less than 6 of them were struck and fell to the ground out of that tree."

"Why didn't our men dig a well?" asked Ned.

"It seems they did afterward, for the place is spoken of as having had a well at the time of the political campaign of 1840, when Harrison was elected President of the United States."

They were now entering the Maumee Bay, and the talk ceased, as all wished to gaze about upon the new scenes as they passed through the

bay and up the river. They visited the ruins of
Fort Meigs, then took carriages and drove three
miles up to Presqu' Isle Hill, alighted there,
and wandered over the battlefield of the Fallen
Timber.

By tea-time they were again on board the
Dolphin, which lay at anchor through the
night in Maumee Bay. It was a delightful
evening, clear and slightly cool on the water,
the stars shining, and a gentle breeze stirring;
and they sat upon the deck for an hour or
more.

"Where are we going to-morrow, papa?"
asked Grace in a pause in the conversation,
which had been running upon the scenes and
adventures of the day.

"To Erie, to view it as the scene of some of
Commodore Perry's doings—if that plan suits
the wishes of those present," returned her
father. "What do you say, mother?"

"That I highly approve," answered Mrs.
Travilla's sweet voice.

"As no doubt we all do," added Mrs. Lilburn.

"Yes," said her husband—"even to the one

who may be suspected of belonging to the British side. But what doings there have you to tell of, captain?"

"It was there that Perry's fleet was made ready for the celebrated Battle of Lake Erie," said Captain Raymond—"Perry's victory was won September 10, 1813."

"Just a few weeks after the fight at Fort Stephenson," remarked Lucilla.

"Yes," said her father; "and at that time the fleet was nearly ready. What we now speak of as Erie was then called Presqu' Isle. The harbor is a large bay, one of the finest on the lake. A low, sandy peninsula juts out some five miles into the lake. It has sometimes been an island, when storms have cleft its neck; and it was a barren sand bank, though now it has a growth of timber upon it. In Perry's time the harbor was a difficult one to enter, by reason of having a tortuous channel, shallow and obstructed by sand bars and shoals."

"Was Erie a city at the time Perry's fleet was built there, papa?" asked Grace.

"No; only an insignificant village, hardly twenty years old; and there were many miles of wilderness, or very thinly populated country, between it and the larger settlements. All the supplies for our men, except the timber for the vessels, had to be brought from a distance, with great labor."

" Captain, was it not at Erie that General Wayne died? " asked Grandma Elsie.

" Yes," he said. " In 1794 General Wayne established a small garrison there and caused a blockhouse to be built at the lake shore of Garrison Hill. He returned there after his victory over the Indians in the Maumee Valley, and occupied a loghouse near the blockhouse, where he died of gout. At his own request he was buried at the foot of the flag-staff."

" Is his grave there now, papa? " asked Elsie.

" No," replied the captain; "his remains were removed to Pennsylvania in 1809. The first building there was a French fort, supposed to have been erected in 1749. I think some of its remains—ramparts and ditches—are still to be seen upon a point overlooking the entrance to the harbor. When Canada became an English possession the fort was allowed to go to decay."

" Why, papa? " asked Ned.

" Because it was no longer needed, my son. The blockhouse built by General Wayne fell into decay and was replaced by a new one in the winter of 1813--14, and a second one was built on the point of the peninsula of Presqu' Isle. The old one was burned by some mischievous person in 1853."

" Well, my dear, I highly approve of your expressed intention to take us to Erie to-morrow," said Violet in a lively tone, as the captain seemed to have come to the end of his account. " I am sure that I for one shall be greatly interested in everything there connected with the past history of our country."

All present seemed to be of the same opinion, and before separating for the night every arrangement was made for an early start next morning.

The yacht was again in motion at an early hour—even before any of her passengers were out of their beds. The sun had not yet appeared above the horizon when the captain was joined upon the deck by Percy Landreth.

" Ah, good-morning, Percy," he said in his usual pleasant tones. " Showing yourself so early a bird makes me fear you have not found your berth as comfortable a couch as could be desired."

" But it is surely none too early for a perfectly healthy fellow to be out, and I was anxious to see the sun rise. I never have seen it come up out of the water."

" Then I advise you to gaze steadily eastward, and you will see it apparently do that in five minutes or less."

Captain Raymond had a strong suspicion that the beautiful sight they presently witnessed was not all the young man had joined him for at that early hour, so he was not surprised when the next moment Percy, turning a rather flushed, embarrassed face toward him, said entreatingly, " Captain, I am sure you are a very kind-hearted man; will you not remove your prohibition of two years ago, and let me tell Miss Lu how I admire and love her? "

" Better not, my young friend," returned the captain pleasantly. " Believe me, you would gain nothing by it, even were her father willing to let her listen to such protestations and engage herself while she is still so young."

"Then she is still free?" Percy asked, his countenance brightening somewhat.

"Yes—heart and hand; and I hope will remain so for some years to come."

"That is some consolation, captain; and it is a great pleasure to be with her, even in the presence of others, and though prohibited to say a word in my own behalf."

"Try to have patience, my young friend," returned the captain, still speaking in a kindly tone; "you are young yet, and though you cannot believe it possible now, the time may come when you will see some other maiden who will be even more attractive to you than my little girl is now."

"I do not know how to believe it, sir," sighed Percy; but at that moment the approach of a light footstep put a sudden end to their talk.

"Good-morning, father, and Percy too! Why, you are out unusually early, are you not?" Lucilla exclaimed, holding out a hand to him. "Is it haste to catch the first glimpse of Erie—not lake but city—that has brought you on deck so soon?"

"Not only that, Miss Lu; it is a delightful

time for being on deck—the sunrise was very beautiful," he said, taking the pretty hand for an instant, and giving it a friendly squeeze; "but you are a trifle too late for that."

"Yes," she said; "but I have seen it a number of times, and may hope to see it many times more on the waters of lakes or oceans."

"I hope you may," he returned pleasantly. "I wish with all my heart that every sort of enjoyment may be yours—now and always."

"Very kind of you," she said with a smile; "but I doubt if it would be best for me to be always free from every sort of trial and trouble. Papa," turning to him, "shall we have our usual stroll back and forth upon the deck— Percy joining us, if he wishes?"

"Yes," her father answered, drawing her hand within his arm; and the three paced back and forth, chatting pleasantly on the ordinary topics of the day till joined by the other members of their party and summoned to the breakfast table.

There was no disappointment in the visit to Erie; it proved quite as interesting as any one of the party had anticipated; the return voyage was delightful. They anchored for the night in the near vicinity of the island where they had landed on first coming to the neighborhood, and whence they received their daily mail.

CHAPTER XII.

"I WONDER if Walter won't be joining us soon?" Lucilla remarked to her father as they walked the deck together the next morning.

"Probably. I should not be surprised to see him at any time," the captain said in reply. "I have sent in for the early mail, and—why here comes the boat now; and see who are in it!"

"Walter and Evelyn! Oh, how glad I am! I don't know how often I have wished she was with us."

"I knew you did, and that you like pleasant surprises, so decided to let this be one."

The boat was already alongside of the yacht, and the next moment its passengers were on deck, the two girls hugging and kissing each other and laughing with delight.

"Now, isn't it my turn, Eva?" queried the captain as they released each other. "Surely I may claim the privilege, since a year or two ago you and I agreed to be brother and sister to each other."

"Yes, sir," laughed Evelyn, making no effort to escape the offered caress.

"And, Lu, as I'm your father's brother I suppose you and I may exchange the same sort of greeting," laughed Walter, giving it as he spoke.

"Well, you have helped yourself; but I do not see any exchange about it," laughed Lucilla; "but, considering your youth, I excuse you for this once."

"As I do also," said the captain. "It isn't every young man I should allow to kiss my daughter; but youth and relationship may claim privileges. Lu, show Eva to her stateroom and see that she has whatever she wants. Walter, the one you occupied last is vacant, and you are welcome to take possession of it again."

"Thank you; I shall be glad to do so," returned Walter, following the girls down the companion-way.

"Quite a mail, I think, this morning, sir," remarked a sailor, handing the captain the mail bag.

Captain Raymond looked over the contents, and found, besides his own, one or more letters for each of his passengers. It was nearing the breakfast hour, and he distributed the letters after all had taken their places at the table.

They were a bright and cheerful party, every-one rejoicing in the arrival of Eva and Walter, the latter of whom had been spending some weeks among the Adirondacks with college-mates, then had joined Evelyn shortly before the last of the family left Crag Cottage, and undertaken to see her safely to the *Dolphin* on Lake Erie.

" As I expected, I am summoned home," said Percy Landreth, looking up from a letter he was reading; " and I am bidden to bring you all with me, if I can by any means persuade you to take the trip. I wish you would all accept the invitation. I can assure you that every-thing possible will be done to prove that we esteem you the most welcome and honored of guests. Cousin Elsie, surely you and Aunt Annis will not think of refusing to spend with us at least a small portion of the time you have allotted for your summer vacation? "

"Certainly I must go with you," said Annis; "those relations are too near and dear to be neglected. My husband will go with me, I know; and you too, Cousin Elsie, will you not?"

"I feel strongly inclined to do so," returned Mrs. Travilla, "and to take the children and grandchildren with me. What do you say to it, captain?"

"It seems to me, mother, that for all of us to go would make a rather large party for our friends to entertain, hospitable as I know them to be," he replied. "Also, there are reasons why I think it would be well for me to remain here on the yacht, keeping Eva, Lu, and Grace for my companions. I flatter myself that I shall be able to give them a pleasant time during the week or two that the rest of you may be absent."

"And you will let me help you in that, sir?" Walter said inquiringly.

"No; my idea was to commit your mother and my wife and children to your care—yours and Cousin Ronald's. He must not have too much of that put upon him."

"Seeing he has grown too auld to be trusted

wi' wark in that line, eh, captain?" remarked Mr. Lilburn in a tone of inquiry.

"Old enough to reasonably expect to be allowed to take his ease, and let women and children be cared for by younger men," returned the captain pleasantly.

"Such as I, for instance," laughed Walter. "Mother, dear, I hope you feel willing to trust me; and that Vi does also."

"My dear boy, I am entirely willing to trust you to do anything in your power for me and any of our dear ones," Grandma Elsie answered with a loving look and smile into her son's eyes.

"And on the journey to Pleasant Plains I shall certainly do my best for you all, Cousin Elsie," said Percy. "But, captain, surely the yacht could do without her owner and his oversight for a fortnight or so. And we can find room for you all; there are several families of us, you must remember, and each of our homes has at least one guest room."

"And you are all very hospitable, I know," returned the captain pleasantly. "Perhaps at some other time I may put that to the proof,

but there are reasons why it does not seem quite
advisable to do so now." The tone of the last
words was so decided that Percy did not think
it advisable to urge the matter any further, and
in a few minutes it was settled that the captain's plan in regard to who should compose the
party to go to Pleasant Plains, and who the one
to remain on the yacht, should be carried out.

Evidently the young girls were well satisfied
with the decision. They had had enough
travel by rail for the present, and life on the
Dolphin would be decidedly restful and enjoyable, for they were delightful companions, the
captain was the best and kindest of protectors
and providers, and there was abundance of
interesting reading matter at hand in the shape
of books and periodicals.

Percy was much disappointed, but did his
best to conceal it, which was the easier because
the others were much taken up with the
necessarily hasty preparations for the little trip.

"I don't want to go without my papa," Ned
said stoutly at first.

"But papa thinks he can't go, and it is for
only a little while, you know," reasoned his

mother. "We expect to come back to papa
and sisters in a few days."

"But, mamma, why don't you and I stay
with him? It's nice here on our yacht and
going about to new places 'most every day."

"So it is, son, but it will be pleasant to see
those relatives who have invited us to their
homes, and to refuse to accept their invitation
would not seem kind."

"But papa does refuse."

"Yes; he must have some good reason which
he has not told us."

"Papa is going to take care of the yacht, and
of Eva and our sisters," said Elsie, joining in
the talk.

They were in their stateroom, Violet putting
together such articles of clothing as she
thought best to take with them on their little
trip.

"But who'll take care of us?" demanded
Ned.

"Uncle Walter, Cousin Ronald, and Cousin
Percy. I'd rather have papa than all of them
put together, but our Heavenly Father will take
care of us, and that is better still."

" Yes, daughter; He will take the best of care of all who put their trust in him; and without his help no earthly creature can keep you from harm," said their father's voice close at hand; and, looking round, they saw him standing in the doorway.

" Yes, papa; and I'm so glad to know it," responded Elsie. " But I do wish you were going along with us to visit those cousins."

" As I do, my dear," said Violet.

" Thank you. I should like it myself, but for certain reasons it seems advisable and best for me to stay behind. Vi, my dear, let me do that packing for you."

The train they had decided to take left early in the afternoon, and they were busy with their preparations until almost the last moment; then they bade the young girls a hasty good-by and left them on the deck, where the captain presently rejoined them, after seeing the departing ones safely on the train and watching it for a moment as it sped rapidly on its way.

" And they are off, are they, father? Well, I hope they will all enjoy themselves greatly, but I am glad we are left here with you," Lucilla said as he rejoined their little group.

" Yes, I saw them off. I hope their visit will prove very enjoyable to them all, and that our stay here will be equally enjoyable to us."

" That is what we are all anticipating, captain," said Evelyn. " I don't know where in the world I should rather pass the next few weeks than on the *Dolphin* with you and these dear girls for company."

" That is pleasant news for us," he returned in kindly tones. " And now what can I do for your entertainment? I am ready to consider suggestions from each of you."

" Don't you think we should take Eva to visit the different islands in this group, papa? " queried Grace.

" Certainly; if she would like to go."

" Very much indeed," said Eva; " I know I shall enjoy going any- and every-where that you may be pleased to take me, or just staying on the yacht lying in one place, if that suits the rest of you."

" We will try that occasionally by way of variety," the captain said with a smile. " Shall we not do that for the rest of this day,—as it is now almost dinner time,—then start off for some other point shortly after breakfast to-morrow morning?"

"Oh, yes, sir!" they all exclaimed; Grace adding, "And, papa, won't you take us to Gibraltar? It is so picturesque that I think it is worth visiting several times."

"Yes, and so are some of the other islands. We will visit any or all of them as many times as you wish."

"Well," said Lucilla, "with taking those little trips now and then, and having books, work,—needlework I mean,—games, and music, I think it will be strange should we find time hang heavy on our hands."

"Yes, indeed," said Evelyn with a sigh of contentment; "I am not in the least afraid of any such calamity."

They talked on, planning various little excursions to one and another of the islands and different points of interest upon the mainland, till summoned to their meal.

"It seems a trifle lonely," Grace remarked as they took their seats about the table.

"Yes," said her father, "but considering how much our absentees are probably enjoying themselves, we won't mind that for a few days."

"Indeed," said Lucilla, "though I shall be glad to see them come back, I think it is really quite delightful to have papa all to ourselves for a few days."

"And for papa to have these young girls all to himself, eh?" laughed the captain. "Well, I won't deny it; and I fully expect the girls to make their companionship quite delightful to me."

"I think we will all do our best in that line," said Evelyn. "It would be strange indeed if we didn't, when you are so very good and kind to us."

"No better, I think, than almost any other gentleman would be in my place," he returned pleasantly. "Now let me help you to some of this fowl. I hope to see you all do full justice to what is set before you."

"If we don't, it will not be the fault of the fare, I am sure," said Evelyn. "Judging by the meals I have taken on board of this vessel, she must have both a good caterer and an excellent cook."

"We have both," said Lucilla emphatically.

"Yes," said Grace. "I wish we could share this dinner with our dear folks who left us a while ago; though perhaps they are getting just as good a meal at Pleasant Plains."

"Yes," said her father, "if all has gone well with them and their train, they are there by this time; and, from what I have heard of the housekeeping of the relatives there, I presume they have been, or will be, set down to as good a meal as this."

"Oh, yes, of course," said Grace; "and that was a very foolish wish of mine. Papa, how shall we spend this evening?"

"I leave that to the decision of my daughters and their guest," he replied. "I shall be happy to do my best to entertain you in any way that may suit your inclinations."

"What may be yours, Eva? Please tell us," said Lucilla.

"I hardly know what to choose," said Evelyn. "Several delightful ways of passing the time have been already spoken of, and I should enjoy any one of them. I hope you will give us some of your music; and if the captain feels inclined to spin us one of his sailor yarns, that would be enjoyable; and I presume a promenade on the deck would be good exercise, helping us to sleep well afterward."

"A very good programme," remarked the captain as she concluded. "I think we will carry it out."

They did so, and, when about to separate for the night, agreed it had been a success, the time having passed very pleasantly.

The next morning found them all in good health and spirits, and the day was spent in little excursions among the islands. The evening brought a mail in which was a letter from Violet to her husband, telling of the safe arrival of her mother, herself, and the other members of their party at their destination, the warm welcome they had received, and the prospect that the few days of their proposed sojourn among the relatives of Pleasant Plains would be passed most agreeably. "There is only one drawback to my enjoyment," she added; "I cannot feel quite content without my husband; and I miss the dear girls too. So I am glad this visit is to be but a short one."

The captain read the greater part of the letter aloud to Eva and his daughters.

"I too am glad their visit is to be short," remarked Grace as he finished, "for I don't like to be without them, though we are having a very delightful time here with our dear, kind father to take care of us and find so many pleasant amusements for us."

"Ah!" he said with a smile. "Where would you like to go to-morrow?"

They discussed the question for a while, and at length decided to visit some of the islands that had been neglected thus far. Then they went on to plan an outing for each weekday of the time they expected the rest of their party to be absent. These they carried out successfully; and each day's mail brought them a graphic report from Violet's pen of the doings among their friends and relatives in Pleasant Plains.

Several family parties were gotten up for their entertainment, and at one of them Cousin Ronald, at Walter's urgent request, exercised his skill in ventriloquism, to the great surprise and delight of the younger folk.

They were quite a large company, assembled in the parlors of Dr. Landreth's house, just after leaving the tea-table. Presently a buzzing bee seemed to be flying about among them, now circling around the head of one person and now flying above that of another. They involuntarily tried to dodge it, and sent searching glances here and there in the vain effort to see just what and where it was. It could not be seen. Presently it was no longer heard, and someone said, "We are rid of it, I think; it seems to have gone out of the window."

But the words were scarcely spoken when there was a scream from the porch, "Oh, I'm stung! and the bee's on me yet! Somebody come and take it off!"

At that the doctor, Walter, and Percy rushed out in response to the entreaty. But the bee's victim seemed to have vanished with wonderful celerity. The porch was entirely deserted.

"Gone! gone already! who can she have been?" exclaimed Percy, glancing about in great surprise.

"I cannot imagine," said the doctor; then catching sight of Walter's face, which told of surpressed mirthfulness, a sudden recollection came to him; and he added, "Ah, I think I understand it," turned, and went back into the parlor.

"Who was it?" asked several voices.

"Nobody, apparently," answered the doctor with a smile; and Percy added, "She had strangely disappeared."

"Well," said a rough voice, seemingly coming from the hall, "if I was a doctor, and a poor woman got badly stung right here in my own house, d'ye think I wouldn't do somethin' fur her?"

"Bring her in here, and I will do what I can for her," replied the doctor.

"Hello here, Bet!" called the voice; "I say, go right along in thar and see what he'll do fur ye."

"What 'll he do? p'raps hurt me worse than the bee has?" snarled a sharp, disagreeable voice. "I guess I won't resk it."

"All right then, Bet, let's go," said the other voice; "'taint our way to stay long where we git nothin' but stings."

A sound as of shuffling footsteps followed, then all was still.

Some of the children and young people ran to the door and windows, hoping to catch sight of the strange couple, but were surprised that they could see nothing of them.

But the bee seemed to have come in again and to be buzzing all about the room—now up near the ceiling, now down about the ears of one and another of the company. There were dodgings and curious glances here and there, exclamations of surprise that the creature was not to be seen as well as heard, till their attention was taken from it by the furious barking of a dog, seemingly on the porch, and mingled with it screams of pain and terror in a childish voice; cries of " Oh, take him off! he's biting me! Oh, oh, he'll kill me! Oh, come quick, somebody, before he kills me! "

Several of the gentlemen present sprang up and rushed out to the rescue, but found all quiet on the porch and neither child nor dog in sight.

For a moment they looked at each other in surprise and perplexity, then a sudden recollection of Cousin Ronald's powers came to one and another, a little amused laugh was exchanged, and they returned to the parlor, looking very grave and as much mystified as even the youngest present.

"Why, who was it? and where did she go to?" asked one of the little girls.

"She was not to be found; nor was the dog," replied Percy. "They seem to have got away very quickly."

"Well, I wish I knew who she was, and whether the dog is after her yet," said Don, his younger brother. "I think I'll go out to the street and see if they are anywhere in sight."

"'Tisn't worth while, little chap; you'll not find 'em," said a voice from the hall which sounded very much like the one that had spoken first.

"Is it your doing? did you bring that dog here?" asked the lad, jumping up and going toward the door.

"Yes," said the voice; "but you needn't worry; she wasn't hurt, though she did do sich tall screamin'. That was jist fer fun and to scare you folks."

"Who are you, anyhow?" asked Don; "and why don't you show yourself? You neither act nor talk like a gentleman."

"Don't I?" asked the voice, ending with a coarse laugh.

"I wouldn't go out there if I were you, little boy; that fellow might do you some harm," said a pleasant voice that seemed to come from a far corner of the room.

Don turned to see who was the speaker, but there was no stranger to be seen, and the voice had certainly not been a familiar one.

"Why," exclaimed the little fellow, "who said that? What's the matter here to-night, that we hear so many folks that we can't see?"

As he spoke, a low whine, that sounded as if made by a young puppy, seemed to come from his pocket. With a startled jump and exclamation, "Oh, how did it get in there?" he clapped his hand upon his pocket. "Why— why, it isn't there! Where is it?" he cried, turning round and round, looking down at his feet, then farther away under chairs and tables. "I can't find it," he said presently, looking much bewildered. "Grandpa, I never saw such things happen in your house before—no, nor anywhere else. What's the matter with me? am I going blind?"

"No, my boy," said the doctor, "we all seem to be as blind as yourself—hearing people talk but not able to see them."

"None so blind as those that won't see," remarked the voice that had spoken last, but this time coming apparently from the doorway. "Here I am, and you are welcome to look at me as closely as you please."

A sudden fierce bark from their very midst seemed to answer her. It was so sudden and sharp that everyone started, and some of the children screamed.

"Nero, be quiet, sir, and walk right out here," said the voice from the hall, and it was answered by a low growl; then all was silent.

"Why, where did he go? and why couldn't we see him?" asked one of the little ones.

"Perhaps we might if we knew where to look and what to look for," said Violet with a smiling glance at Cousin Ronald.

"But where's that little pup that was in my pocket?" cried Don, as if with sudden recollec-

tion, and glancing about the floor. " I can't
see how in the world he got there, nor how he
got out again."

Just as he finished his sentence the puppy's
whine was heard, seeming to come from behind
the large armchair in which Cousin Ronald was
seated.

" There he is now! " cried Don. " I wish
he'd come out of that corner and let us all see
him."

" Perhaps he will if you invite him," said the
old gentleman, rising and pushing his chair a
little to one side.

Don made haste to look behind it. " Why,
there's nothing there! " he cried. " What does
go with the little scamp? "

" Perhaps he's afraid of you, Don, so gets out
of sight as fast as possible," said Percy.

" Then why did he get in my pocket? " asked
Don; then added quickly, " But maybe he
wasn't there, for I couldn't find him, though I
clapped my hand on it the instant I heard his
whine." Just then the whine, followed by a
little bark, seemed to come from the farther
side of the room, and the children hurried over

there to make a vain search for the strangely
invisible puppy.

"Where did it go to?" they asked. "How
could it get away so fast? and without anybody
seeing it?"

"Well, it isn't here, that's certain," said one.
"Let's look in the hall."

They rushed out there, then out to the porch,
looking searchingly about everywhere, but finding nothing.

"Oh, it must have got away into the
grounds," cried one. "Let's look there," and
they ran down the path to the gate, off across
and around the grounds—some in one direction, some in another. But it took only a few
minutes to satisfy them that no little dog was
there; and they trooped back to the house to
report their inability to find it.

They were all talking at once, discussing
their failure in eager, excited tones, when again
that strange, gruff voice was heard in the
hall.

"Say, youngsters, what have you done with
my little dog? He's of fine stock, and if you
don't hand him over right away—why, I'll know

the reason why, and it won't be good fur ye, I can tell ye."

"We didn't take him," answered Don; "we've never seen him at all—no, not one of us; and if we had, we wouldn't have done him a bit of harm."

Just as Don pronounced the last word, a shrill little bark sounded out from behind Cousin Ronald's chair.

"Why, there he is now!" exclaimed Don, hurrying to the spot. "Why, no, he isn't! How does he get away so fast?"

"He seems to be an invisible dog, Don," said his brother Percy; "and, if I were you, I wouldn't let him trouble me any more."

"No; but I've set out to find him, and I don't mean to give it up," replied the little fellow.

"That's right, Don," laughed his father. "I'm pleased to see that you are not easily discouraged."

"But he might as well be, for there's no dog thar," said the voice from the hall. "He's a plucky little feller, but he'll not find that thar dog if he looks all night."

"I guess I'll find you then," said Don, running to the door and looking searchingly about the hall. "Well, it's the queerest thing!" he exclaimed. "There's nobody here—nobody at all!"

"Is the boy blind, that he goes right past a body and never sees him?" asked the voice; and Don turned quickly to see the speaker, who seemed close behind him. But no one was there, and Don looked really frightened. Cousin Ronald noticed it, and said in kindly tones, "Don't be scared, sonny, it was I who spoke; and I wouldn't harm you for all I am worth."

"You, sir?" said Don, looking utterly astonished. "How could it be you? for the fellow was over here, and you are over there."

"No; I only made it sound so," Mr. Lilburn said with an amused laugh; "and I must confess that I have been doing all this screaming, scolding, and barking just to make a bit of fun for you all."

At that the children crowded around the old gentleman, eagerly asking how he did it and what else he could do.

"I can hardly tell you how," he said, "but

perhaps I can show some other specimens of my work." He was silent for a moment, seemingly thinking. Then a loud, rough voice said: "Hello there, youngsters, what are you bothering with that stupid old fellow for? Why don't you leave him and go off to your sports? It would be a great deal more fun."

The children turned toward the place from which the voice seemed to come, but saw no one. They were surprised at first, laughed, asking, "Was that you, Uncle Ronald?"

"Nobody else," he said with a smile.

"Oh, hark! there's music!" cried one of the little girls; and all listened in silence.

"It is a bagpipe, playing a Scotch air," said Percy, who was standing near their little group.

"What queer music!" said one of the little girls when it had ceased; "but I like it. Please, Uncle Ronald, make some more."

Several tunes followed, and then the children were told they had monopolized their Uncle Ronald long enough and must leave him to the older people for a while.

"But you'll do some more for us some other

time, won't you, Uncle Ronald?" asked one of the little girls as they reluctantly withdrew from his immediate neighborhood.

"Yes, little dear, I will," he answered kindly.

And he did entertain them in the same way a number of times during his short stay in their town.

CHAPTER XIII.

"WELL, papa, where shall we go, or what shall we do, to-day?" asked Grace one bright September morning as they sat about the breakfast table on board the *Dolphin*.

"Let me hear the wishes of all three of you in regard to that matter," he said in his accustomed pleasant tones. 'Evelyn, what have you to say? Have you any plans you would like carried out?"

"No, sir, thank you," she replied. "I shall be perfectly contented to stay on the *Dolphin* or go anywhere you and the girls wish."

"I think we have seen all the points of interest about here," he said. "However, if you would like to pay a second visit to any one of them you have only to say so."

Just as the captain spoke a sailor came in with the mail-bag.

"Ah," said Grace, "I hope there is a letter

from Mamma Vi saying that she and the rest will be here to-day or to-morrow."

"Yes, so do I," said Lucilla. "We have had a lovely time while they have been away, but I shall be delighted to have them back again."

"Yes," said her father, "here is a letter from her to me." Then opening and glancing over it: "They are coming back to-day, and may be expected by the train that gets into Cleveland near tea-time. I must go for them; and you, Lucilla—you and Grace—may see that everything about the cabin and staterooms is in good order for their comfort and enjoyment."

"Yes, papa, we will," they answered promptly, Lucilla adding with a merry look, "We will do the work ourselves if that is your wish."

"Oh, no," he said; "I only meant that you should oversee it, and make sure that nothing is left undone which would add to their comfort."

"I wish we had some flowers to ornament the rooms with," said Grace.

"You shall have," replied her father. "I have sent for some by the man who has gone to the city to do the marketing."

"Oh, that's good!" exclaimed Lucilla. "Papa, I believe one may always trust you to think of everything."

"I am not so sure of that," he said with a smile. "But it is very well for my daughters to think so."

"I do, papa," said Grace. "Lu can't have any more confidence in you than I have."

"Nor than I," said Evelyn. "And I am very proud of the privilege accorded me some time ago of considering you my brother, captain."

"Ah? I think I am the one to feel honored by the relationship," he returned laughingly.

"We will start for home pretty soon, father, won't we?" asked Grace.

"I presume so; we will consult the others on that subject when they come. Are you growing homesick?"

"Almost," she answered, but in a cheery tone. "I have enjoyed our outings on the Hudson and here ever so much, but ours is such a sweet home that I begin to long to see it again."

"Well, dear child, I hope to be able to gratify that wish before long," he replied in kindly, affectionate tones. "I am very glad you love your home."

"It is certainly worthy of her love," said Evelyn. "I don't know a more delightful place; yet it would not be half so charming without the dear people who live in it."

"It certainly would not be to me without the wife and children who share it with me," said the captain.

They had not left the table long when flowers were brought aboard in variety and abundance, and they had a very enjoyable time arranging them in vases, and placing those where they could be seen to the best advantage.

"There," said Lucilla when their labors were completed; "they will do very well while the *Dolphin* stands still, but if she takes to rolling, as I have known her to do at times in the past, we'll have to empty the water out of the vases or it will empty itself where it is not wanted at all '

"Yes," said her father, "but I think you may confidently expect her to remain stationary at least until to-morrow morning. No one is likely to care to start on the homeward journey before that time."

"I wish they were here now," said Grace; "but we have hours to wait before we can hope to see them."

"Have patience, daughter," her father said in cheerful tones. "The time will soon pass; and, to make it go faster, shall we not row over to one of the islands and have a stroll on the beach?"

The girls all seemed pleased with that proposal; the captain gave the order to have the boat made ready, and in a few moments they were on their way. It was just the kind of a day to make such a little excursion very enjoyable, and in a couple of hours they returned, feeling in fine health and spirits and ready for either work or play.

Captain Raymond saw them safely on board, presently followed them himself, and read aloud an entertaining book while they busied themselves with bits of needlework. Soon dinner was announced; quite a while was spent at the table, and shortly after they left it, the boat was again in requisition to take the captain to the city and bring him and the returned travellers back to the yacht.

The time of his absence seemed rather long to the waiting girls; but when at last the boat came into sight, and they perceived that it held all the expected ones, they were overjoyed, and when the deck was reached the embraces exchanged were warm and loving.

"This seems very like a home-coming," said Violet. "We have had a delightful time with our Pleasant Plains cousins, yet are glad to be again on our own floating home."

"Yes," said her mother; "especially as we hope it will soon carry us to our still dearer ones in the Sunny South."

"I am ready to start for them to-morrow, mother, if you wish it," the captain said in his pleasant way. "I presume you have all seen enough, for the present at least, of this part of our country."

He looked inquiringly at Annis as he spoke.

"I am ready to go or stay, as the others

wish," she said. " It is now late in September, and the excessive summer heat will surely be over by the time we reach our journey's end. What are your opinions and feelings on the subject, my dear? " turning to her husband.

" I care but little one way or the other, so that I have my wife with me, and she is satisfied," returned Mr. Lilburn gallantly.

" And that, I presume, is about the way with these younger folk," remarked the captain, glancing around in a kindly way upon them.

" Yes, captain," said Evelyn; " we are all ready, I am sure, to go or stay, as seems best to you."

" One can always find enjoyment wherever you are, father," said Lucilla.

" Yes, indeed," said Grace. " But now, good folks, please all come down to the saloon and see our preparations for your arrival." She led the way, the others following, and on reaching the saloon and seeing its wealth of adornment, they gave such meed of praise as greatly gratified the young decorators.

" Ah, it is nearly tea-time," said Grandma Elsie at length, consulting her watch; " and I at least need to make some preparation in the way of ridding myself of the dust of travel by rail," and with that all the returned travellers retired to their staterooms for the few minutes that remained ere the summons to the tea table.

On leaving the table, all repaired to the deck, where they spent the evening in pleasant chat, finding much to tell each other of the doings and happenings of the days of their separation.

They closed their day as usual, with a service of prayer and praise and the reading of the Scriptures, then all except the captain retired to their staterooms.

But it was not long before Lucilla, as usual, stole back to the deck for a good-night bit of chat with her father. She found him walking the deck and gazing earnestly at the sky.

"Is there a storm coming, father?" she asked.

"I think there is," he answered, "and probably a heavy one. I think it should make a change in our plans, for it may last several days. In that case we will be safer over there in Put-in Bay, lying at anchor, than we would be out in the lake."

"Then you will go over there, won't you, father?" she asked.

"I think I shall," he said. "It really matters but little whether we get home as speedily as the voyage can be made, or not until a week or two later."

"I am glad of that," she returned; "and as we have an abundance of books and games,—plenty of everything to make the time pass quickly and pleasantly,—I think we need not mind the detention."

"I agree with you in that," he said, "and I am very glad that our dear absentees got here safely before the coming of the storm."

"Then you don't apprehend any danger?" she said inquiringly.

"No; not if we are at anchor in the bay yonder. Well, you came to say good-night to your father in the usual way, I suppose?"

"Yes, sir; but mayn't I stay with you for a little while? I am not at all sleepy, and should enjoy pacing back and forth here with you a few times."

"Very well, daughter," he returned, taking her hand and drawing it within his arm.

They walked to and fro for a time in silence. It was broken at length by Lucilla. " To-morrow is Friday, but you don't think it would be unlucky to start on a journey for that reason, father? "

" No, child; it is the coming storm, and not the day of the week, that seemed portentous to me. I have sailed more than once on Friday, and had quite as prosperous a voyage as when I had started on any other day of the week."

" It seems to me absurd and superstitious," she said, " and I know Grandma Elsie considers it so. Papa, isn't that cloud spreading and growing darker? "

" Yes; and I think I must give orders at once to get up steam, lift the anchor, and move out into the bay. Say good-night, now, and go to your berth."

Violet, arrayed in a pretty dressing gown, stepped out of her stateroom door into the saloon as Lucilla entered it. " Are we about starting, Lu? " she asked. " I thought I heard your father giving an order as if preparations for that were going on." Lucilla replied with an account of what she had seen and heard while on deck. "But don't be alarmed, Mamma Vi," she concluded; "father thinks there will be no danger to us lying at anchor in Put-in Bay, and I think we will be able to pass the time right pleasantly."

"So do I," said Violet; "but it will be sad if he has to expose himself to the storm. However, I suppose that will hardly be necessary if we are lying at anchor. Yes, I think we are a large enough and congenial enough company to be able to pass a few days very pleasantly together, even though deprived of all communication with the outside world."

"So we won't fret, but be glad and thankful that we can get into a harbor before the storm is upon us, and that we have so competent a captain to attend to all that is needed for our safety and comfort," returned Lucilla. "But I must say good-night now, for papa's order to me was to go to my berth."

The *Dolphin* was soon in motion, and within an hour lying safely at anchor in Put-in Bay. When her passengers awoke in the morning, quite a severe storm was raging, and they were well pleased that it had not caught them upon the open lake; and though Grandma Elsie had grown anxious to get home for her father's sake, she did not fret or worry over a providential hindrance, but was bright and cheerful, and ever ready to take her part in entertaining the little company.

For three days the ladies and children scarcely ventured upon deck; but, with books and work and games, time passed swiftly, never hanging heavy on their hands. Mr. Lilburn, too, caused some amusement by the exercise of his ventriloquial powers.

It was the second day of the storm, early in the afternoon, and all were gathered in the saloon, the ladies busy with their needlework, the gentlemen reading, Elsie and Ned playing a quiet game. Walter had a daily paper in his hand, but presently threw it down and sat with his elbow on the table, his head on his hand, apparently in deep thought. He sighed wearily, and then words seemed to come from his lips.

"Dear me, but I am tired of this dull place! —nothing to see, nothing to hear, but the raging of the storm!"

"Why, Walter!" exclaimed his mother, looking at him in astonishment; but even as she spoke she saw that he was as much astonished as herself.

"I didn't make that remark, mother," he laughed. "I am thankful to be here, and enjoying myself right well. Ah, Cousin Ronald, I think you know who made that ill-sounding speech."

"Ah," said the old gentleman with a sad shake of the head, "there seems to be never a rude or disagreeable speech that is not laid to my account."

Then a voice seemed to come from a distant corner: "Can't you let that poor old mon alone? It was I that said the words you accuse him of uttering."

"Ah," said Walter; "then show yourself, and let us see what you are like."

"I am not hiding, and don't object to being looked at, though I am not half so well worth looking at as some of the other people in this room."

"Well, that acknowledgment shows that you are not vain and conceited," said Walter.

"Who would dare call me that?" asked the voice in angry, indignant tones.

The words were quickly followed by a sharp bark, and then the angry spitting of a cat, both seeming to come from under the table.

Little Elsie, who was sitting close beside it, sprang up with a startled cry of "Oh, whose dog and cat are they?"

"Cousin Ronald's," laughed Ned, peeping under the table and seeing nothing there.

At that instant a bee seemed to fly close to the little boy's ear, then circle round his head, and he involuntarily dodged and put up his hand to drive it away. Then he laughed, saying in mirthful tones, "Oh, that was just Cousin Ronald, I know!"

The older people were looking on and laughing, but Lucilla started and sprang to her feet with an exclamation of affright as the loud, fierce bark of a seemingly ferocious big dog sounded close to her ear. Everybody laughed, she among the rest, but she said pleadingly: "Oh, don't do that again, Cousin Ronald! I didn't know I had any nerves, but I believe I have."

"Well, daughter, don't encourage them," her father said in kind and tender tones, taking her hand in his as he spoke, for she was close at his side, as she was pretty sure to be whenever she could manage it.

"I am truly sorry if I hurt those nerves, Lu," said the old gentleman kindly. "I meant but to afford amusement, and shall be more careful in the future."

"Do some more, Cousin Ronald; oh, please do some more, without scaring Lu or anybody," pleaded Ned.

"Ned, Ned, it's time to go to bed," said a voice seeming to come from the door of the stateroom where the little boy usually passed the night.

"No, sir, you're mistaken," he answered; "it won't be that for two or three hours yet."

"Captain," called a voice that seemed to come from overhead, "please come up here, sir, and see if all is going well with the vessel."

Captain Raymond looked up. "I think I can trust matters to you for the present, my men," he said. "We are in a safe harbor and have little or nothing to fear."

"Papa, did somebody call you?" asked Ned.

"I rather think Cousin Ronald did," answered the captain; "but I don't intend to go to the deck to find him, or answer his call to it, while he sits here."

"No; what business has he to treat you so?" said a voice that sounded like a woman's. "He ought to be glad to see you sit down and take a rest occasionally."

"So he is," said Cousin Ronald, speaking in his natural tone and manner. "He is always glad to have such busy folks take a bit o' rest."

"But please don't you take a rest yet, Cousin Ronald; we want you to make some more fun for us first—if you're not too tired," said Ned, in coaxing tones.

"I am more than willing, laddie," returned the old gentleman pleasantly, "for fun is ofttimes beneficial, particularly to little chaps such as you."

"I am bigger than I used to be," said Ned, "but I like fun quite as well as I ever did."

"Very strange," said Lucilla, "very strange that a grave old man such as you should care for fun."

"Yes, but my sister Lu likes it, and she's older—a great deal older than I am," returned the little fellow, looking up into her face with eyes that sparkled with fun.

At that she laughed and gave him a kiss.

"Yes, I am a great deal older than you, and so you ought to treat me with great respect," she said.

"Ought I, papa?" he asked, turning to their father.

"It would be quite well to do so, if you want the reputation of being a little gentleman," replied the captain, regarding his little son with a smile of amusement.

But at that instant there came a sound as of a shrill whistle overhead, followed by a shout in stentorian tones: "Hello! look out there! Ship ahoy! Do you mean to run into us? If we get foul of each other somebody may be sent to Davy Jones' locker."

Everybody started, and the captain rose to his feet, a look of anxiety coming over his face.

But Cousin Ronald gave him a roguish look.

"I wouldn't mind it, captain," he said.

"It's only a false alarm. I doubt if there is any vessel near us."

The captain reseated himself, while Grace exclaimed with a sigh of relief, "Oh, I am so glad it was but a false alarm! A collision would be so dreadful, either to us or to the people on the other vessel, and maybe to both."

"Oh, it was just you, was it, Cousin Ronald?" laughed Ned. "Please do some more."

At that instant there was a loud squeak, as of a mouse that seemed to be on his own shoulder, and he started to his feet with a loud scream: "Oh, take it off, papa! Quick, quick!"

Everybody laughed; and Lucilla said teasingly, "I'm afraid you are not fit to be a soldier yet, Neddie boy."

"Maybe I will be by the time I'm tall enough," he returned rather shamefacedly.

"Yes, son, I believe you will," said his father. "I don't expect a son of mine to grow up to be a coward."

"I might have known it was Cousin Ronald, and not a real mouse, on my shoulder," remarked the little fellow with a mortified air; "but I didn't think just the first minute."

"Cousin Ronald on your shoulder?" laughed Lucilla. "I don't think he could stand there; and his weight would be quite crushing to you."

"Of course it would. He couldn't stand there at all," laughed Ned.

"No," said Mr. Lilburn, "it would be much more sensible for me to take you on my shoulder."

"Papa takes me on his sometimes," said Ned, "but not so often now as he used to when I was a little boy."

"Ha, ha, ha! what are you now, sonny?" asked a voice that seemed to come from a distance.

Ned colored up. "I'm a good deal bigger now than I was once," he said.

"And hoping to grow a good deal bigger yet," added his father, smiling down into the little flushed, excited face.

"Yes, papa, I hope to be as big as brother Max, or you, some of these days," returned the child.

"Don't be in a hurry about growing up," said the voice that had spoken a moment before.

" Grown folk have troubles and trials the little ones know nothing about."

" But the grown-ups may hope to do more in the world than the little ones," said Walter.

" Is that why you are growing up, Uncle Walter? " asked Ned.

" That's why I am glad to grow up," replied Walter.

" Like papa? "

" Yes; and like grandpa and other good men."

" Well, I want to be a man just like my own dear papa," said the little fellow, looking with loving admiration up into his father's face.

" That's right, bit laddie, follow closely in his footsteps," said the voice, that seemed to come from that distant corner.

But now came the call to the supper table, and so ended the sport for that day.

CHAPTER XIV.

IT was still raining heavily when the Sabbath morning dawned upon Lake Erie and Put-in Bay. But the faces that gathered about the breakfast table of the *Dolphin* were bright and cheery. Everybody was well and in good spirits.

"This is a long storm, but I think will be over by to-morrow," remarked the captain as he filled the plates.

"The time has not seemed long to me," said Annis, "for even though deprived of the pleasure of being on deck we have been by no means a dull party."

"No, not by any means, and Mr. Lilburn has made a great deal of fun for us," said Evelyn.

"And feels well repaid by the evident enjoyment of the little company," he said, glancing around upon them with a pleasant smile.

"But of course that kind of sport won't do for to-day," said Walter; "and I presume it is too stormy for anybody to go ashore to attend church." With the concluding words he turned toward the captain inquiringly.

"Quite so," was the reply. "We will have to content ourselves with such a service as can be conducted on board."

"Which will probably be quite as good and acceptable as many a one conducted on land," said Mr. Lilburn. "I have greatly enjoyed the few I have been privileged to attend on this vessel in the past."

"And I," said Grandma Elsie; "we are as near the Master here as anywhere else; and when we cannot reach a church, we can rejoice in that thought—in the remembrance that he is just as near us here as anywhere else."

"We will have a sermon, prayers, and hymns this morning, and a Bible class this afternoon, won't we, papa?" asked Grace.

"Yes," he said; "but our guests must feel entirely free to attend our services or not as they feel inclined."

"This one will feel inclined to attend," said Walter.

"This one also," added Evelyn; "she will esteem it a privilege to be allowed to do so."

"As I do," said Lucilla. "Father always makes a Bible lesson, and any kind of religious services, interesting and profitable."

"I always enjoy them," said Violet, "and I know Grace and the little folks do. Is not that so, Elsie and Ned?" Both gave a prompt assent, and Grace said: "There is no kind of service I like better. So I do not feel tempted to fret over the stormy weather."

"Ah," said the captain with a smile, "I am well content with the views and feelings expressed by my prospective audience. We will hold our services in the saloon, beginning at eleven o'clock."

Accordingly, all—including the crew—gathered there at the appointed hour, listened attentively to the reading of an excellent sermon, and united in prayer and praise.

In the afternoon they gathered there again, each with a Bible in hand, and spent an hour in the study of the Scriptures.

As in the morning service, the captain was their leader.

"Let us take the sea for our subject," he said, "and learn some of the things the Bible says of it. Cousin Ronald, what can you tell us or read us on the subject?"

"There is a great deal to be said," replied the old gentleman. "It is spoken of in the very first chapter of the Bible—'the gathering together of the waters called the seas.' In the twentieth chapter of Exodus we are told, 'In six days the Lord made heaven and earth, the sea and all that in them is'; and in the fifth verse of Psalm ninety-five, 'The sea is his, and he made it.' The Hebrews called all large collections of waters seas. The Mediterranean was the Great Sea of the Hebrews.

"In the Temple was a great basin which Solomon had made for the convenience of the priests; they drew water out of it for washing their hands or feet, or anything they might wish to cleanse.

"The Orientals sometimes gave the name of sea to great rivers overflowing their banks— such as the Nile, the Tigris, and the Euphrates, because by their size, and the extent of their overflowing, they seemed like small seas or great lakes. The sea is also taken for a multitude or deluge of enemies. Jeremiah tells us the sea is come up upon Babylon. But I am taking more than my turn. Let us hear from someone else."

" From you, Cousin Annis," the captain said, looking at her.

" No, I have not studied the subject sufficiently," she said, " but doubtless Cousin Elsie has."

" Let me read a verse in the last chapter of Micah," responded Grandma Elsie, and went on to do so:

" ' He will turn again, he will have compassion upon us; he will subdue our iniquities; and thou wilt cast all their sins into the depths of the sea.'

" What a gracious and precious assurance it is! " she said. " What is cast into the sea is generally supposed to be lost beyond recovery —we do not expect ever to see it again; so to be told that our sins are cast there imports that they are to be seen and heard of no more."

" Because Jesus died for us and washed them all away in his precious blood? " asked Little Elsie softly.

"Yes, dear, that is just what it means," replied her grandmother.

Evelyn's turn had come, and she read: "'And before the throne there was a sea of glass like unto crystal.' Cruden says," she continued, "that it probably signified the blood of Christ, whereby our persons and services are made acceptable to God; and that it was called a sea in allusion to the molten sea of the Temple. Also that it is represented as a sea of glass like unto crystal, to denote the spotless innocence of our Lord Jesus Christ, in his sufferings; that his was not the blood of a malefactor, but of an innocent person."

"One suffering not for his own sins, but for the sins of others," sighed Grandma Elsie. "What wondrous love and condescension; and, oh, what devoted, loving, faithful servants to him should we ever be!"

"We should, indeed," said the captain, then motioned to Lucilla that it was her turn.

"'He shall have dominion also from sea to sea, and from the river unto the ends of the earth,'" she read. Then turning over the leaves, "That was in the Psalms," she said;

"and here in Zachariah the prophecy is repeated in almost the same words, 'And his dominion shall be from sea even to sea, and from the river to the ends of the earth.' The dominion of Christ, is it not, father?"

"Certainly; it can be no other," he said. "Now, Grace, it is your turn."

"Mine is in the New Testament," she said— "the eighth chapter of Matthew, beginning with the twenty-third verse. 'And when he was entered into a ship, his disciples followed him. And behold there arose a great tempest in the sea, insomuch that the ship was covered with the waves: but he was asleep. And his disciples came to him and awoke him, saying, Lord save us: we perish. And he saith unto them, Why are ye fearful, O ye of little faith? Then he arose and rebuked the winds and the sea; and there was a great calm. But the men marvelled, saying, What manner of man is this, that even the winds and the sea obey him.'"

"It is such a pretty story," said Little Elsie. "How kind Jesus was never to get angry, though they waked him out of his sleep when he must have been so very, very tired. He might have scolded them, and asked didn't they know they couldn't drown while he was with them in the ship."

" Yes," her father said; " and let us learn of him to be patient, unselfish, and forgiving."

It was Walter's turn, and he read: " ' And when even was come, the ship was in the midst of the sea, and he alone on the land. And he saw them toiling in rowing; for the wind was contrary unto them; and about the fourth watch of the night he cometh unto them, walking upon the sea, and would have passed by them. But when they saw him walking upon the sea, they supposed it had been a spirit, and cried out; for they all saw him and were troubled. And immediately he talked with them, and saith unto them, Be of good cheer: it is I; be not afraid.' "

" This is mine," said Elsie. " ' And he went forth again by the seaside: and all the multitudes resorted unto him, and he taught them.' "

It was Ned's turn, and he read: " And he began again to teach by the seaside: and there was gathered unto him a great multitude, so that he entered into a ship, and sat in the sea; and the whole multitude was by the sea on the land.' "

" I think this was a very nice lesson," Elsie said as they closed their books. " I shall think of it often while we are on the sea. This— Lake Erie—is as much of a sea as the Lake of Tiberias or Sea of Galilee, isn't it, papa? "

" I think so," he said; " and in a few days we are likely to be on a real sea—the great Atlantic Ocean."

" And God can take care of us there just as well as anywhere else, can't he, papa? " asked Ned in a tone that was half inquiry, half assertion.

" Certainly, my son, he is the creator of all things, the ruler of all the universe, and ' none can stay his hand or say unto him, What doest thou? ' "

" Papa," said Ned, " mightn't I ask him to stop this storm, so we could go right on home? "

" You can ask him, son, to do it if he sees best, but you must be willing that he should not do what you wish if he does not see best. God knows what is best for us, and we do not, but often desire what would be very bad for us."

"Well, papa, I'll try to ask that way," said the little boy. "But I'm very tired of these dark, rainy days, and of staying still in one place where we don't see anything, and I hope our Heavenly Father will let us start away to-morrow."

"Neddie, dear," said his grandmother, "don't forget what a blessing it has been that we had this safe harbor close at hand when the storm was coming, so that we could run right into it. If we had been away out upon the lake our vessel might have been wrecked."

"Yes, grandma, I am glad and thankful for that," he said; "I'm afraid I was grumbling just now, but I don't intend to do so any more."

"I'll be glad when good weather comes again," remarked Elsie, "but I have really enjoyed myself right well these days that we have had to spend in the cabin; Cousin Ronald has made a great deal of fun for us."

"Yes, indeed!" exclaimed Ned earnestly, and laughing as he spoke; "it was lots of fun to hear people talking and animals barking and squealing when they weren't really here at all. Now, what are you all laughing at?" he asked in conclusion.

"At your animals," said Lucilla. "I understood that all the barking and squealing you talk about was the doing of a very nice old gentleman."

"Yes," said Ned a trifle shamefacedly; "but please don't be hurt or affronted, Cousin Ronald; I didn't know how to say it any better."

"No, sonny, and you meant it all right," the old gentleman answered pleasantly. "I am very glad to be able to furnish amusement for so good and lovable a bit of a kinsman as yourself."

"Thank you, sir. I like that word—kinsman," said the little boy, regarding Mr. Lilburn with sparkling eyes. "It means a relation, doesn't it?"

"Yes, just that, laddie. Your grandmother and mother are of my kin, and that makes you so too. I hope you are not ill-pleased to own so auld a cousin?"

"No, indeed, sir," said Neddie earnestly; "and I'll try to behave so well that you won't ever feel ashamed to own me for your kin."

"It will be a great surprise to me if ever I do feel my relationship to you and yours a disgrace, laddie," the old gentleman said with a smile. Then, turning to Violet, "Could not you give us a bit o' sacred music, cousin?" he asked. "It strikes me 'twould be a fitting winding-up of our services."

"So I think," said the captain; and Violet at once took her place at the instrument.

"Mamma," said Grace, "let us have 'Master, the Tempest is Raging.' We can all sing it, and it is so sweet."

"Yes," said Violet.

The others gathered around her, and together they sang:

> " ' Master, the tempest is raging!
>   The billows are tossing high!
>   The sky is o'ershadowed with blackness!
>   No shelter or help is nigh!
>   Carest thou not that we perish?
>   How canst thou lie asleep,
>   When each moment so madly is threatening
>   A grave in the angry deep?

Chorus :
 " ' The winds and the waves shall obey thy will,
    Peace, be still!
  Whether the wrath of the storm-tossed sea,
  Or demons, or man, or whatever it be,
  No waters can swallow the ship where lies
  The Master of ocean, and earth, and skies ;
    They all so sweetly obey thy will,
      Peace, be still!   Peace, be still!
    They all so sweetly obey thy will,
      Peace, peace, be still!

 " ' Master, with anguish of spirit
    I bow in my grief to-day;
  The depths of my sad heart are troubled;
    Oh, waken and save, I pray!
  Torrents of sin and of anguish
    Sweep o'er my sinking soul;
  And I perish! I perish, dear Master,
    Oh, hasten and take control!

Chorus :
 " ' The winds and the waves shall obey thy will, etc.

 " ' Master, the terror is over,
    The elements sweetly rest;
  Earth's sun in the calm lake is mirrored,
    And heaven's within my breast;
  Linger, O blessed Redeemer!
    Leave me alone no more;
  And with joy I shall make the blest harbor,
    And rest on the blissful shore.

Chorus :
 " ' The winds and the waves shall obey thy will,' " etc.

CHAPTER XV.

The *Dolphin's* passengers retired early to their staterooms on that stormy Sunday night; that is, all of them except the captain and Lucilla. He was on the deck, and she sat in the saloon, reading and waiting for a little chat with her father before seeking her berth for the night. Presently she heard his approaching footsteps, and, closing her book, looked up at him with a glad smile.

"Ah, daughter, so you are here waiting for me as usual," he said in his kind, fatherly tones; and, taking a large easy-chair close at hand, he drew her to a seat upon his knee. "You haven't sat here for quite a while," he said, passing his arm about her and pressing his lips to her cheek.

"No, sir; and I am very glad to be allowed to do it again, big and old as I am," she returned with a smile that was full of love and pleasure. "Oh, I am so glad—so glad every day that God gave me to you instead of to somebody else. I thank him for it very often."

"As I do," he said; "for I consider my dear eldest daughter one of God's good gifts to me."

"Whenever I hear you say that, father, I feel ashamed of all my faults and follies and want—oh, so much—to grow wiser and better."

"I too need to grow better and wiser," he said; "and we must both ask daily and hourly to be washed from our sins in the precious blood of Christ—that fountain opened for sin and for uncleanness.

> "'There is a fountain filled with blood,
>   Drawn from Immanuel's veins;
> And sinners, plunged beneath that flood,
>   Lose all their guilty stains.'"

"Papa, I love that hymn, and am thankful to Cowper for writing it," she said.

"And so am I," he returned. "Oh, what gratitude we owe for the opening of that fountain! for the love of Christ that led him to die that painful and shameful death of the cross—that we might live. 'The love of Christ which passeth knowledge.'"

They were silent for a little; then he said,

"It is growing late, daughter; it is quite time time that this one of my birdlings was in her nest. Give me my good-night kiss and go."

"Can I go to you on the deck in the morning, papa?" she asked as she prepared to obey.

"That depends upon the weather," he answered. "If it is neither raining nor blowing hard, you may; otherwise, you may not."

"Yes, sir; I'll be careful to obey," she said with a loving smile up into his face.

All seemed quiet within and without when she awoke in the morning, and dressing speedily she stole out through the cabin, and up the stairway, till she could look out upon the deck. Her father was there, caught sight of her at once, and drew quickly near.

"Good-morning, daughter," he said; "you may come out here, for it is not raining just now, and the wind has fallen."

"Is the storm over, father, do you think?" she asked, hastening to his side.

"The worst of it certainly is, and I think it will probably clear before night."

"So that we can start on our homeward journey?"

" Yes," he answered; " but it will not be well
to leave this safe harbor until we are quite certain of at least tolerably good weather."

" No, none of us would want to run any risk
of shipwreck," she said; " and there isn't really
anything to hurry us greatly about getting back
to our homes."

" Nothing except the desire to see them and
our dear ones there," he said; " and to delay
that will be wiser than running any risk
to bring it about sooner."

As he spoke he drew her hand within his
arm, and they paced the deck to and fro for
some time; then it began to rain again, and he
bade her go below.

" Still raining, I believe," remarked Mr. Lilburn as they sat at the breakfast table.

" Yes," replied the captain; " but I think it
will probably clear by noon."

" And then we will start on our return journey, I suppose? " said Walter.

" Yes," said the captain, " that seems best,
and I believe is according to the desire of all my
passengers. It is your wish, mother, is it not? "
turning to Grandma Elsie.

"I should like to get home soon now," she replied; "but shall not fret if we are still providentially detained."

The rain had ceased by the time they left the table, so that they were able to go on deck, take some exercise, and get a view of their surroundings.

By noon the indications were such that the captain considered it entirely safe to continue their journey. So steam was gotten up, and they were presently out of the harbor and making their way across the lake in the direction of the Welland Canal. Before sunset all the clouds had cleared away; the evening was beautiful, and so were the days that followed while they passed down the St. Lawrence River and out through the Gulf, then along the Atlantic coast, stopping only once, to let Walter leave them for Princeton.

It was quite a long voyage, and a very pleasant one; but everyone was glad when at length they reached the harbor of the city near their homes. They were expected, and found friends and carriages awaiting their coming.

Mr. Hugh Lilburn had come for his father

and Annis, Edward Travilla for his mother and Evelyn, and the Woodburn carriage was there to take the captain and his family to their home.

"It is delightful to have you at home again, mother," Edward said as they drove off; "we have all been looking forward to your coming —from grandpa down to the babies that can hardly lisp your name."

"It is most pleasant to be so loved," she said with a joyful smile, "especially by those who are so dear as my father, children, and grandchildren are to me. Are all well at Fairview?"

"Yes, and looking forward, not to your return only, but to Evelyn's also. Lester was very busy, so asked me to bring her home to them; which I was very ready to do."

"And for which I feel very much obliged," said Evelyn. "I shall be very glad to get home, though I have had a delightful time while away."

They soon reached Fairview, and her welcome there was all she could desire. Grandma Elsie was warmly welcomed too, but did not alight. She felt in much too great haste to see her father and the others at Ion.

On her arrival she found her daughter Rosie there also, and her presence added to the joy of the occasion.

Dinner was ready to be served, and Harold and Herbert had just come in from their professional rounds, so that the family reunion was almost complete. They missed Walter, but were glad to think of him as well, happy, and busied with his studies; and Elsie and Violet, though not just there, were near enough to be seen and conversed with almost any day. So it was altogether a cheerful and happy reunion, as was that of the family at Fairview.

Woodburn held no welcoming relatives for the Raymonds, but theirs was a glad homecoming, nevertheless. The grounds were in beautiful order, as was the dwelling under Christine's skilful management; and the dinner that awaited the returned travellers was abundant in quantity and variety, and the cooking such as might have found favor with an epicure.

"I think we are most fortunate people," said Violet as they sat at the table. "I know it isn't every family that can come home after weeks of absence to find everything in beautiful order and the table furnished with luxuries as is this one."

"Very true, my dear," said the captain; "we certainly have a great deal to be thankful for."

"Yes, papa, it is very pleasant to be at home again," said Elsie; "and when dinner is over mayn't we go all around and look at every one of the rooms, upstairs and down?"

"If you want to make the circuit of the house, I have no objection," he said.

"Yes, I do, papa," she answered. "I feel very much as if the rooms are old friends that I'm quite fond of."

"The schoolroom as well as the rest?" he asked with a look of amusement.

"Yes, indeed, papa, for you make lessons so pleasant that I'd be very, very sorry to be shut out of that room. Wouldn't you, Neddie?"

"Course I would," exclaimed Ned. "I love to be with papa, and I like the nice lessons. Papa often tells us a great deal that is very interesting."

"I am glad you think so," said his father.

"We will visit the schoolroom, as well as the others, after we have finished our dinners."

"Will we have school to-morrow, papa?" asked Elsie.

"No; you may have the rest of the week for play, and we will begin lessons on Monday if nothing happens to prevent."

"We will take up our studies again, papa, just as the little ones do, will we not?" asked Lucilla.

"Meaning Grace and yourself, I suppose?" he said inquiringly, and with a look of amusement.

"Yes, sir; except Evelyn, we are your only other pupils just now."

"You can both begin when the younger ones do, if you like," he replied; and Grace said, "You may be quite sure we will like to do so, papa."

"Papa, when will Brother Max come home?" asked Ned.

"I think we may expect him about the last of next January," was the reply.

"And how soon does January come, papa?"

"This is October: November comes next, then December, and next after that is January."

"Oh, such a long while!" sighed Ned. "I want to see Max so badly that I don't know how to wait."

"Pretty much the way papa feels about it," returned his father.

"And as we all do," said Violet. "I wish the dear fellow had chosen work that could be done at home."

"But somebody must go into the navy, my dear," said his father. "A good navy is very necessary for the safety of the country."

"That is true," she returned; "and I know of no more honorable employment."

"And employment of some kind we all should have. I know of nothing more ignoble than a life of idleness. It is sure to tempt to something worse. 'Satan finds some mischief still for idle hands to do.'"

"Yes," said Violet, "and the Bible bids us to be 'diligent in business, fervent in spirit, serving the Lord.'"

"And in the fourth commandment we are bidden, 'Six days shalt thou labor and do all thy work.' It makes no exception; recognizes no privileged class who may take their ease in idleness."

"Yet there are times when one is really weary, that rest is right, are there not?" said Violet. "I remember that at one time Jesus said to his disciples, 'Come ye yourselves apart into a desert place, and rest a while.'"

"Yes; there are times when rest is very necessary, and by taking it one is enabled to do more in the end."

"And we have just had a nice long rest," said Grace; "so ought to be able to go to work earnestly and make good progress in our studies."

"So I think," said Lucilla; then added laughingly, "and I'm glad father doesn't turn me out of the schoolroom because I've grown so big and old."

"You are still small enough, and young enough, to demean yourself as one under authority," remarked the captain in pleasant tones; "otherwise you would not be admitted to the schoolroom among my younger pupils."

Just then a rather discordant voice was heard

calling, " Lu, Lu, what you 'bout? Polly
wants a cracker."

" You shall have one presently, Polly," Lucilla answered.

" Oh, let's all go up there and see her," said
Ned as they rose and left the table.

" Yes, we may as well begin there to make
our circuit of the house," said his father; and
they all hastened up the stairway to the apartments of Lucilla and Grace.

" I think Polly is glad to see us," said Elsie,
as they stood for a moment watching her while
she ate.

" A good deal more pleased to see and taste
the cracker," said her father. " I doubt if par-
rots ever have much affection to bestow on anyone."

" Well, Polly," said Lulu, " nobody cares
particularly for your affection; but in spite of
your coldness and indifference, you shall have
plenty to eat."

" Your rooms are in good order, daughters,"
said the captain, glancing about them. " I
think Christine is an excellent housekeeper."

" So do I, father," said Lucilla. " We have

only to unpack our trunks and put their contents in their proper places, and all will be as
neat and orderly as before we left home."

"Yes, but we are going to visit the other
parts of the house first," said Grace; "or we'll
have to do it alone, which wouldn't be half so
much fun as going along with papa and the
rest."

They finished their inspection quickly, then
set to work at their unpacking and arranging,
laughing and chatting merrily as they worked.

Violet, in her rooms, with Elsie and Ned to
help or hinder, was busied in much the same
manner. The captain was in the library examining letters and periodicals which had accumu-
lated during his absence, when he was
interrupted by the announcement that Mr.
Dinsmore had called to see him.

"Mr. Dinsmore?" he said inquiringly.

"Yes, sah; Mr. Chester. Here am his
kyard."

"Ah, yes; just show him in here."

The two greeted each other cordially, and
Chester was invited to take a seat, which he
did.

"I am making you an early call, captain," he said. "I knew you were expected to-day, and heard, perhaps an hour ago, that you had actually arrived. I have, as you requested, kept a lookout for that escaped convict who threatened your daughter at the time of his trial. He has not yet been caught, but as I cannot learn that he has been seen anywhere in this neighborhood, I hope he has given up the idea of wreaking vengeance upon her."

"I hope so, indeed," returned her father; "but I shall be very careful never to let her go from home unattended."

"I am glad to hear you say that, sir," said Chester; "and I shall be very happy if I may sometimes be permitted to act as her escort. You may not always find it entirely convenient to undertake the duty yourself."

"Thank you for your offer; I may sometimes be glad to avail myself of it," was the reply.

They chatted a while longer, then Chester rose as if to take his leave.

"Don't go yet," said the captain. "My wife and daughters will join us presently, and feel glad to see you. Stay and take tea with us, and give us all the news about the family at The Oaks."

"Thank you," returned Chester, sitting down again. "We are all quite well, Syd busy with her preparations for going South to join Maud and Dick."

"Ah! she leaves soon?"

"I think before very long; but the exact time is not set yet."

"You will feel lonely—robbed of both your sisters."

"Yes, sir," Chester returned with a slight smile. "I should greatly prize a sweet young wife, who would much more than fill their places."

"Ah, yes; but this is one of the cases where it is best to make haste slowly, my young friend," the captain returned in a pleasant tone.

"I am feeling a little uneasy lest Percy Landreth or someone else may have got ahead of me," Chester said inquiringly, and with an anxious look.

"No; her father wouldn't allow any such attempt, and it is quite sure that his daughter is still heart-whole. And as I have told you be-

fore, if either suit is to prosper, I should rather
it should be yours—as in that case she would
not be taken far away from me."

"That is some consolation, and she is well
worth waiting for," said Chester in a tone of
resignation.

"So her father thinks," said the captain.

Just then there was a sound of wheels on the
drive.

"The Roselands carriage," said Chester,
glancing from the window; and both he and the
captain rose and hurried out.

They found the whole Roselands family
there—Calhoun and his wife and children;
Dr. Arthur, his Marian, and their little Ronald.

Violet and her children, with Lucilla and
Grace, had hastened down to receive them, and
warm greetings were exchanged all around.

Chester took particular pains to get possession of a seat near Lucilla, and had many questions to ask in regard to the manner in which
she had spent the long weeks of her absence
from home—for long, he averred, they had
seemed to him.

"Well now, they didn't to me," laughed Lucilla; "on the contrary, I thought them very short; time fairly flew."

"And was so filled with interesting occurrences that you hardly thought of your absent friends?"

"Oh, yes; I did think of them, occasionally even of you, Chester," she said in sportive tone. "Really, I do wish you could have seen and enjoyed all that we did. Were you moping at home all the time?"

"Not all the time; much of it found me very busy; and for a fortnight I was away on a boating excursion with some friends."

"I am glad of that, for I am sure you needed some rest. Sometimes I think you are too hard a worker. Don't forget the old saying that 'All work and no play makes Jack a dull boy.'"

But there the talk was interrupted by another arrival—the carriage from The Oaks, bringing all that family, including Chester's sister Sydney. They were on their way to Ion to welcome Grandma Elsie home, so made but a short call.

The Roselands people were urged to stay to

tea, but declined, and presently took their leave. But they had scarcely gone, when Violet's brothers Harold and Herbert came, and they stayed to tea. They were bright and genial as usual; Chester, too, was gay and lively; and so altogether they constituted a blithe and merry party.

The evening brought the families from Ashlands, Pinegrove, and The Laurels, and the next day those from Fairview, Beechwood, and Riverside. Rosie expressed herself as charmed with her new home, and insisted upon having them all there to tea with her mother and old Mr. and Mrs. Dinsmore. The other relatives she had already entertained, she said; and she was planning to have all at once at no very distant day.

"Surely we can wait for that, Rosie," said the captain, "and content ourselves with a call upon you and a sight of your pretty home, leaving the greater visit to the time you speak of."

"No, Brother Levis, I won't be satisfied with that," she said. "I want you all to take tea with us to-morrow evening."

"Are you not willing that we should, father?" asked Lucilla.

"Yes, if you wish to do so," he replied; and as all expressed themselves desirous to accept the invitation, they did so; and they were so well and hospitably entertained that everyone was delighted. They returned home rather early in the evening, on account of the little ones. Violet took them upstairs at once, and Grace went to her room, so that Lucilla and her father were left alone together, as so often happened early in the evening. She followed him into the library, asking, "Haven't you some letters to be answered, father? and shall I not write them for you on the typewriter?"

"I fear you are too tired, daughter, and had better be getting ready for bed," he answered, giving her a searching but affectionate look.

"Oh, no, sir," she said; "I am neither tired nor sleepy; and if I can be of any use to my dear, kind father, nothing would please me better."

He smiled at that, lifted the cover from the machine, and they worked busily together for the next half-hour or more. When they had finished, "Thank you, daughter," he said; "you are such a help and comfort to me that I hardly know what I should ever do without you."

"Oh, you are so kind to say that, you dear father," she returned, her eyes shining with joy and filial love. "I often say to myself, 'How could I ever live without my dear father?' and then I ask God to let you live as long as I do. And I hope he will."

"He will do what is best for us, daughter," returned the captain in moved tones; "and if we must part in this world, we may hope to meet in that better land where death and partings are unknown."

"Yes, papa, the thought of that must be the greatest comfort when death robs us of our dear ones."

He took her hand, led her to a sofa, and, seating her by his side, put his arm about her, drawing her close to him. "I have something to say to you, daughter," he said in low, tender tones.

She gave him a rather startled, inquiring look, asking, "About what, papa?"

"You remember the bit of news—in regard to the escape of a convict—which hastened our departure for the North some months ago?"

"Yes, sir; and has he not been caught and returned to his prison?"

"No; and I have reason to think he is somewhere in this neighborhood, probably bent on evil deeds, perhaps among them some harm to my daughter, whose testimony helped to send him to prison for the burglary committed here. I tell you this, my child, as a warning to you to be very careful how you expose yourself to possible danger from him."

"Yes, papa, I will; but you know I never go outside the grounds without a protector, because you long ago forbade my doing so."

"Yes; but now you must not go everywhere even inside of them; avoid the wood, and keep near the house unless I am with you."

"Yes, sir; I will obey. But, father, he may come into the house in the night. You know he did before."

"Yes, I remember; and I have arranged to have watchmen—armed men—patrolling the grounds near at hand; so that if he makes such an attempt it will be at the risk of his life. It is wise and right for us to take all possible precautions, then trust calmly and securely in the protecting care of our Heavenly Father. Try to do so, dear child, and do not lie awake in fear and trembling."

"I will not, if I can help it, father," she said.

"I will remember the sweet words of the Psalmist, 'The salvation of the righteous is of the Lord; he is their strength in the time of trouble. And the Lord shall help them and deliver them: he shall deliver them from the wicked, and save them, because they trust in him.'"

"Yes," he said, "trust in the Lord and he will deliver you. 'According to your faith be it unto you.' Have confidence in your earthly father too. We will have the doors open between our rooms, and if anything alarms you in the night run right to your father for protection and help."

"I will, dear papa," she said; "and, oh, with a kind, all-wise and all-mighty Heavenly Father, and so dear and wise an earthly one, I can lie down in peace and sleep as sweetly as ever I did."

"I hope so, dear child. And I think I hardly need caution you to keep all this from our timid, nervous Grace; and the younger ones also."

"They shall not learn it from me, papa," she said; "I will do what I can to keep them all in ignorance of the danger that seems to threaten."

She kept her word, and a week slipped by without any further evidence of the near vicinity of the convict.

CHAPTER XVI.

Lucilla and Grace rode out every day on their ponies, always accompanied by their father, sometimes by Violet also, though the latter generally preferred a drive in the carriage, taking her children with her. And Lucilla, being stronger than Grace, would, if she had occasion, go a second time when it suited her father to go with her. Chester Dinsmore came often to the house, and sometimes joined them in their rides; for he was keeping a vigilant watch for traces of the escaped convict who was known to cherish so great an enmity to Lucilla.

Chester made no lover-like advances to the girl he so coveted, because so far he had been unable to win her father's consent, but he was glad to seize every opportunity to be with her and do his best to make himself necessary to her happiness. So far she seemed to look upon him as a pleasant friend, but nothing more; yet he was not altogether discouraged. He thought her worth long and patiently waiting for and much effort to win.

One afternoon of a beautiful October day the captain remarked that he had an errand to the town, and asked who would like to go with him.

"I should like it," said Violet, "but cannot very well, as I am to have a dress fitted."

"And you, Grace, had so long a ride this morning that you are too tired for another, I presume?" her father said inquiringly.

"Yes, papa," she said; "though I love to ride with you for my escort, I believe I am too tired for anything but a rest and nap this afternoon."

"So, father, I'm afraid you can not secure any better company than mine," remarked Lucilla with an amused little laugh.

"So it seems," he said. "Well, since I can do no better, I will accept yours if it be offered me."

"It is, then, sir; and I promise to be ready at any hour you appoint."

"We will start early, shortly after leaving

the table, that we may get home before dark," he said, with a look and smile that seemed to say her company would be very acceptable.

The roads were good, the horses fresh and lively; and they had a delightful ride going to Union, and also returning—until near home.

Chester had joined them, and the captain, seeing something in a field belonging to his estate that he wanted to examine, told the others to ride on and he would follow very shortly.

They did as he requested, but had not gone more than a hundred yards when a man suddenly rose from behind a bush, pistol in hand, and fired, taking aim at Lucilla. But Chester had seized her bridle at the instant of the rising of the figure, and backed both her horse and his just in time to escape the shot which whizzed past them over the horses' heads. Chester instantly snatched a pistol from his pocket, took aim at the miscreant, and fired at the same instant that the scoundrel sent a second shot in their direction. Then the wounded murderer dropped and lay still as death, while Chester dismounted, reeled, and fell by the roadside—dead, as Lucilla thought in wild distress. She dismounted and went to him.

" Oh, Chester, Chester, where are you hurt? " she cried in sore distress.

He seemed to be unconscious, and she did not know whether he was dead or alive. But the next moment her father was beside her with two or three of the men employed on the estate.

" Oh, papa, he has died for me! " she cried, hot tears streaming down her face.

" No, he is not dead, daughter," her father said in tender tones. " But we will never forget the service he has done us this day."

" No, sah, Mars Chess 's alive, sho 'nuff," said one of the men; " an' we'll git Doctah Arthur or Doctah Harold or Herbert here, and dey'll cure him up, sho's a gun."

" Yes; go after one of them as fast as you can. Catch Mr. Chester's horse and ride him; then take him to The Oaks and leave him there. Mr. Chester must be carried carefully into Woodburn and nursed there—as long as he needs it. Well, is that fellow living or dead? "

he asked of one of the men who had climbed the fence and was stooping over the prostrate form of the convict.

" Dead, cap'ain; dead as anything. He won' do no mo' mischief in dis worl'."

" Poor wretch! " sighed the captain. Then he gave directions to the men to go to the house and bring from there a cot-bed on which they could carry the wounded man without increasing his suffering by unnecessary jolts and jars.

All this time Lucilla was standing by her father's side, trembling and weeping.

" Oh, papa, I'm afraid he has given his life for mine," she sobbed.

" I hope not, dear child," he said; " he is living, and I hope his wound will not prove mortal. In saving my daughter's life he has done me a service that I can never repay, and I hope it is not to cost him his own life."

At that moment Chester's eyes opened, and Lucilla never forgot the look of joy and love that he gave her.

" Thank God, you are alive and unhurt," he said, in a low tone and gasping for breath.

"But, oh, Chester, you are so terribly injured," she sobbed. "I am afraid you are suffering very much."

"Don't weep. I can bear it," he said.

"My dear fellow, don't try to talk any more now," said the captain. "I have sent for one or more of our doctors, and here come my men with a cot-bed to carry you to Woodburn, where you must stay until you are entirely well."

"You are most kind, captain," murmured the half-fainting young man, "but——"

"No, no; don't try to talk. I can never repay you for saving my child," the captain said with emotion.

Chester's only reply was a look at Lucilla that seemed to say that nothing could be too costly if done for her.

"And, oh, what a debt of gratitude I owe you!" she exclaimed. "I can never repay it."

"Dearest, I would give my life for yours at any time," he responded.

The words and the look that accompanied them were a revelation to Lucilla. The look of a moment before had surprised her, and raised a question in her mind as to just what she was

to him; but there was no mistaking this. He
loved her; loved her well enough to die in her
stead.

But the men were at hand with the cot, and
under the captain's direction the wounded man
was lifted carefully and tenderly, laid upon it,
and carried to the house, the captain on his
horse, and Lúcilla on her pony, following
closely.

In the meantime Violet and Christine had
made ready a bed in the room occupied by Captain Raymond at the time of his injury from
being thrown by Thunderer, and there they
laid Chester, just as Drs. Arthur Conly and
Harold Travilla arrived, having come with all
possible haste at the summons sent by the captain.

Violet, Lucilla, and Grace, seated on the
veranda, anxiously awaited the doctors' verdict.

It was Harold who brought it at length.

"The wound is a serious one," he said in
reply to their looks of earnest inquiry; "but we
have succeeded in removing the ball, and do
not by any means despair of his life."

"Oh, I hope he will recover," sobbed Lucilla;

"for if he does not, I shall always feel that he has given his life for mine."

"But it was through no fault of yours, Lu; you were not in the least to blame," said Harold soothingly. "And you can pray for his recovery; we all will. But don't worry and fret; for that will only make you unhappy and perhaps ill, and do him no good."

"That is good advice, Harold," said her father, who had joined them just in time to hear it; "worrying about what may happen only unfits us for present duty, and makes us less able to meet the trouble when it comes."

"That scoundrel is dead?" Harold said half inquiringly.

"Yes; Chester's shot, fired simultaneously with his, was fatal. He dropped, and, I think, died almost instantly. Poor wretch! the world is well rid of him; but what has become of his soul?"

"Oh, I don't believe Chester meant to kill him outright!" exclaimed Lucilla; "I believe he was only thinking of saving my life."

"And to kill the wretch who was trying to kill you seemed to be the only way of doing that," said Harold. "But I must go," he added, rising. "We think we must have a professional nurse for Chester. I happen to know of one who has just finished an engagement, and I am going for her at once, if you do not object to having her in the house, Vi—you or the captain."

Both promptly replied that they would be glad to have her there, and Harold at once set out upon his errand.

For some days Chester lay half unconscious, and apparently hovering upon the brink of the grave, while those who loved him watched and waited in intense anxiety. Then a change came, and the doctors said he would recover. Lucilla heard it with a burst of weeping that seemed more like the expression of despair and sorrow than the relief and joy that really filled her heart.

It was her father who told her the glad news, and they were alone together in the library. He drew her into his arms and held her close.

"It is altogether glad news, dear child," he said; "Chester is a Christian and a young man of talent who will lead a useful life, I think, and it would have been a bitter sorrow to have had him fall a victim to that worthless, cowardly convict."

"And in my defence," she sobbed. "Oh, papa, it makes my heart ache to think how he has suffered because of risking his life in the effort to save mine."

"Yes; I am very grateful to him—so grateful that I feel I can refuse him nothing that he may ask of me—even though it should be the the hand of my dear eldest daughter."

She gave him a look of surprise, while her cheek grew hot with blushes.

"You know that he wants it—that he loves you. He made it very plain as we stood by him in the road soon after he fell."

"Yes, sir; and I have thought of it very often since. It surprised me very much, for I had never thought of him as a lover."

"And how is it now?" asked her father, as she paused; "do you care for him at all? can you give him any return of affection?"

"Papa," she said, hiding her blushing face on his shoulder, and speaking in so low a tone that he scarcely caught the words, "I seem to have learned to love him since knowing of his love to me and that he had almost, if not quite, t..rown away his own life to save mine. But you are not willing that he should tell his love? —not willing to give me to him, however much he may desire it?"

"I am too grateful to him to refuse him anything he may ask for—even to the daughter who is so dear to me that I can scarcely bear the thought of resigning her to another."

"Oh, father, how could I ever endure to be parted from you!" she cried, clinging more closely to him.

"Dear child," he said, holding her close; "we will make it a condition that you shall not be taken away to any distance. And, in any event, you are still too young to leave your father; you must remain single and live with me for at least a year or two longer."

"Oh, I am glad to hear you say that!" she said. "Papa, has Chester said anything to you?" she asked.

"Yes; he has several times begged permission to tell you of his love and try to win yours.

I have hitherto refused because of your youth, but shall now let him have his way."

.   .   .   .   .   .

"You are improving fast, and I hope will soon be able to be up and about again," the captain said to Chester, a few days later.

"Yes," said the young man, "I begin to feel as if I had taken a new lease of life and—ah, captain, if I could at last find such favor in your eyes that you would consent to——" His sentence was left unfinished.

"To letting you tell your tale of love?" Captain Raymond asked with a smile.

"Just that, sir. I cannot help fearing it may prove useless, but—anything is better than suspense; which I feel that I have hardly strength to endure any longer."

"Nor can I any longer ask that of you, since you have freely risked your life for hers," returned the captain with emotion. "Your nurse being out just now, this is a good opportunity, and I will bring my daughter to you and let you have it out," he concluded in a jesting tone, and left the room as he spoke.

Lucilla happened to be near at hand, and

almost immediately her father had brought her to Chester's bedside. She knew nothing of the talk that had been going on, yet, remembering her conversation with her father a few days before, came to the bedside blushing and slightly embarrassed.

"I am very glad you are better, Chester," she said, laying her hand in his as he held it out to her. "What a hard, hard time you have had, and all because you risked your life to save mine."

"I'm not sorry I did, and would do it again without a moment's hesitation," he said. "Oh, Lu, if I could but tell you how dear you are to me! Can you not give me a little love in return?"

"Oh, Chester, how could I help it, when you have almost died for me?" she asked, bursting into tears.

"Don't be distressed over that, dear one," he returned, pressing the hand he still held in his, then lifting it to his lips. "Will you be mine?" he asked imploringly.

"If papa consents, and you will never take me far away from him."

"He has consented, and I will never take you anywhere that you do not want to go. We will live here among our own dear ones as long as the Lord spares us to each other."

As he finished he drew her down to him, and their lips met.

"We belong to each other now," he said, "and I hope both of us will always rejoice that it is so."

"I hope you will, my dear children," said the captain. "And now, Chester, get well as fast as you can. I cannot give Lucilla up entirely to you for a year or more yet, but you can visit her here every day if you like."

So the young couple were engaged, and very happy in each other, Chester making rapid improvement in health from the hour when he was assured of the prosperity of his suit.

The betrothal was soon made known to all the connection, and seemed to give satisfaction to everyone. Sydney had gone South before Chester's encounter with the escaped convict, and she and Maud wrote their congratulations. Frank was pleased, and came oftener than before to Woodburn. Lucilla's bosom friend,

Evelyn, approved of the match, and hoped Lu would be a happy wife, but thought she herself would prefer to live single. Grace was half-pleased, half-sorry because she did not seem quite so necessary to her sister's happiness as before.

Captain Raymond did not.at all enjoy the thought of even a partial giving up of his daughter to the care of another, but tried to forget that the time was coming when it must be done. That Max was expected home in a few weeks made that difficult task somewhat easier. All were looking joyfully forward to that happy event.

If you are interested in continuing reading the
Elsie Dinsmore Series, by Martha Finley

Sovereign Grace Publishers, Inc.
P.O. Box 4998
Lafayette, IN 47903
Phone: (765) 429-4122
Fax: (765) 429-4142

FAMILY LINEAGE

HORACE
HORACE DINSMORE SR.
HORACE DINSMORE JR. (ELSIE'S FATHER)
HORACE HOWARD (NEPHEW)

ELSIE
ELSIE GRAYSON DINSMORE
ELSIE DINSMORE TRAVILLA (ELSIE'S DAUGHTER)
ELSIE TRAVILLA (DAUGHTER OF E.D.T.)

ROSE
ROSE ALLISON DINSMORE
ROSE DINSMORE (DAUGHTER)
ROSE TRAVILLA (GRANDDAUGHTER TO R.A.D.)
ROSE HOWARD (NIECE TO R.A.D.)

EDWARD
EDWARN TRAVILLA SR.
EDWARD TRAVILLA JR. (EDDIE)
EDWARD HOWARD SR.
EDWARD HOWARD JR. (NED)
EDWARD ALLISON

ARTHUR
ARTHUR DINSMORE
ARTHUR HOWARD (NEPHEW)

FAMILY LINEAGE

WALTER
WALTER DINSMORE
WALTER CONLEY (NEPHEW)
WALTER HOWARD (NEPHEW)
WALTER TRAVILLA (GRAND NEPHEW)

HERBERT
HERBERT CARRINGTON
HERBERT CARRINGTON (NEPHEW)
HERBERT TRAVILLA (NAMESAKE)

HAROLD (HARRY)
HAROLD ALLISON
HARROLD CARRINGTON SR.
HAROLD CARRINGTON JR. (HARRY)
HAROLD TRAVILLA (NAMESAKE II.A.)
HARRY DUNCAN

ARCHIE
ARCHIE CARRINGTON
ARCHIE ROSS (NEPHEW)

SOPHIE
SOPHIE ALLISON CARRINGTON
SOPHIE ROSS (NIECE)

DAISY
DAISY ALLISON
DAISY CARRINGTON (NIECE)

www.ingramcontent.com/pod-product-compliance
Lightning Source LLC
Chambersburg PA
CBHW060001100426
42740CB00010B/1358